St. Mary's Parish Hymnal

Unless otherwise noted, all music and text can be found in the Public Domain.

Music selections compiled by Allison Stanley –Director of Music, St. Mary's Ballston Spa, NY

Nihil Obstat granted by The Most Reverend Bishop Edward Scharfenberger, Bishop of Albany, NY on October 31, 2024.

All Glory Be to Jesus Christ!
This collection of hymns would not have been made possible without the support of the enthusiastic parishioners of St. Mary's, choir members, and mentors in my life.

Special thanks to Paul Jernberg, Jr. who generously gave permission to incorporate *Mass of St. Philip Neri* into this hymnal. His prayerful compositions elevate the Liturgy and bring the hearts of the faithful to the Wedding Feast of the Lamb.

Thank you also to the *Foundation of the Dominican Liturgical Center* in Kraków, Poland. They "wholeheartedly" agreed to let their compositions and arrangements to be included in this compilation of edifying hymns.

My prayer is that you will experience the transforming effects that music brings to the Sacred Liturgy and help you to enter even deeper into this great mystery.

Allison Stanley

Mass of St. Philip Neri

Lord, Have Mercy

Kyrie, Eleison

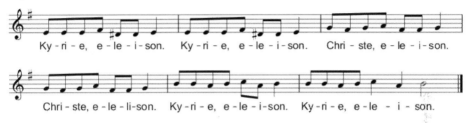

Glory to God

Holy, Holy, Holy

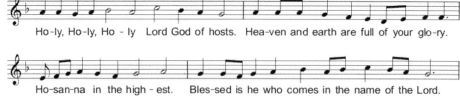

Text © 2010 ICEL
Music © 2011 (& 2018 revision) Paul Jernberg

Memorial Acclamation

A.

We pro-claim You Death, O Lord, and pro-fess Your Re-sur-rec-tion, un-til You come a-gain.

B.

When we eat this Bread and drink this Cup, we pro-claim Your Death, O Lord, un-til You come a-gain.

C.

Save us, Sa-vior of the world, for by Your Cross and Re-sur-rec-tion, you have set us free.

Amen

A-men.   or: A-men, a-men, a-men.

Lamb of God

Lamb of God, you take a-way the sins of the world, have mer - cy on us.

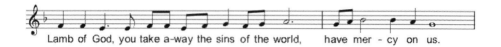
Lamb of God, you take a-way the sins of the world, have mer - cy on us.

Lamb of God, you take a-way the sins of the world, grant us peace.

Text © 2010 ICEL
Music © 2011 (& 2018 revision) Paul Jernberg

Hymns

1

'Tis Good Lord To Be Here

1. 'Tis good, Lord, to be here! Thy glo-ry fills the night; Thy face and gar-ments, like the sun, Shine with un-bor-rowed light.
2. 'Tis good, Lord, to be here. Thy beau-ty to be-hold Where Mo-ses and E-li-jah stand, Thy mes-sen-gers of old.
3. Ful-fill-er of the past! Prom-ise of things to be! We hail Thy Bod-y glo-ri-fied, And our re-demp-tion see.

J. Armitage Robinson   SWABIA, 6.6.8.6. (S.M.)

2

A Thrilling Voice by Jordan Rings

1. A thrill-ing voice by Jor-dan rings, Re-buk-ing guilt and dark-some things: Vain dreams of sin and vi-sions fly; Christ in his might shines forth on high.
2. Now let each bur-dened soul a-rise That sunk in guilt and wound-ed lies; See! The new Star's re-ful-gent ray Shall chase dis-ease and sin a-way.
3. The Lamb de-scends from heav'n a-bove To par-don sin with fre-est love: Or such in-dul-gent mer-cy shown With tear-ful joy our thanks we own.

Vox clara ecce intonat, 10th c.   WINCHESTER NEW, 8.8.8.8. (L.M)
Tr. John M. Neale

Adoro Te Devote

1. A - dó - ro te de - vó - te, la - tens Dé - i - tas,
2. Vi - sus, ta - ctus, gu - stus in te fál - lo - tur,
3. In cru - ce la - té - bat so - la Dé - i - tas,
4. Pla - gas, si - cut Tho - mas, non in - tú - e - or:
5. O me - mo - ri - á - le mor - tis Dó - mi - ní,
6. Pi - e pel - li - cá - ne, Je - su Dó - mi - ne,
7. Je - su, quem ve - lá - tum nunc a - spí - ci - o,

1. Quae sub his fi - gú - ris ve - re lá - ti - tas:
2. Sed au - dí - tu so - lo tu - to cré - di - tur:
3. At hic la - tet si - mul et hu - má - ni - tas:
4. De - um ta - men me - um te con - fí - te - or:
5. Pa - nis vi - vus vi - tam prae - stans hó - mi - ni,
6. Me im - mún - dum mun - da tu - o sán - gui - ne,
7. O - ro fi - at il - lud quod tam sí - ti - o:

1. Ti - bi se cor me - um to - tum súb - ji - cit,
2. Cre - do quid - quid di - xit De - i Fí - li - us:
3. Am - bo ta - men cre - dens at - que cón - fi - tens,
4. Fac me ti - bi sem - per ma - gis cré - de - re,
5. Prae - sta me - ae men - ti de te ví - ve - re,
6. Cu - jus u - na stil - la sal - vum fá - ce - re
7. Ut te re - ve - lá - ta cer - nens fá - ci - e,

1. Qui - a te con - tém - plans to - tum dé - fi - cit.
2. Nil hoc ver - bo ve - ri - tá - tis vé - ri - us.
3. Pe - to quod pe - tí - vit la - tro paé - ni - tens.
4. In te spem ha - bé - re, te di - lí - ge - re.
5. Et te il - li sem - per dul - ce sá - pe - re.
6. To - tum mun - dum quit ab o - mni scé - le - re.
7. Vi - su sim be - á - tus tu - ae gló - ri - ae. A - men.

St. Thomas Aquinas

ADORO TE DEVOTE, 11.11.11.11.

Again We Keep this Solemn Fast

1. Again we keep this solemn fast, As taught by ways of ages past; The fast to all men known, and bound In forty days of yearly round.
2. The law and seer that were of old In diverse ways this Lent foretold, Which Christ, all seasons' King and Guide, In after ages sanctified
3. More sparing therefore let us make The words we speak, the food we take, Our sleep and mirth and closer barred Be every sense in holy guard.

ERHALT UNS HERR, 8.8.8.8. (L.M)

Ex moe docti mystio, Attr. Pope St Gregory the Great
Tr. John M. Neale, alt

6

All Creatures of Our God and King

1. All crea-tures of our God and King Lift
2. Thou rush-ing wind that art so strong Ye
3. Thou flow-ing wa-ter, pure and clear, Make

1. up your voice and with us sing, Al-le - lu - ia! Al-le-
2. clouds that sail in Heav'n a - long, O praise him! Al-le-
3. mu - sic for thy Lord to hear, O praise him! Al-le-

1. lu - ia! Thou burn-ing sun with gold-en beam, Thou
2. lu - ia! Thou ris-ing moon, in praise re - joice Ye
3. lu - ia! Thou fire so mas-ter-ful and bright, That

1. sil - ver moon with soft - er gleam!
2. lights of eve-ning, find a voice! O praise him! O
3. giv - est man both warmth and light.

praise him! Al-le-lu - ia! Al-le-lu - ia! Al-le-lu - ia!

Cantico di fratre sole, Attr. St. Francis of Assisi;
Tr. William H. Draper

LASST UNS ERFREUN, 8.8.8.8. (L.M)
with Alleluias

7

All Glory, Laud and Honor

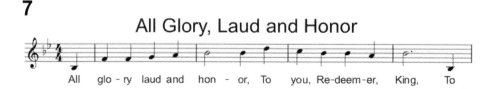

All glo-ry laud and hon - or, To you, Re-deem-er, King, To

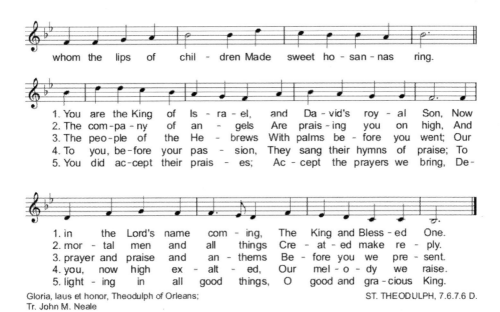

All Hail the Power of Jesus' Name

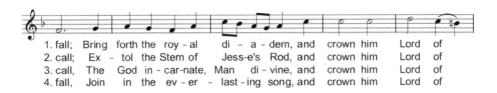

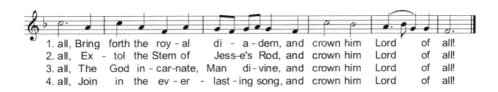

Edward Perronet, alt John Rippon

CORONATION, 8.6.8.6. (C.M.)
with repeat

9. All People That on Earth Do Dwell

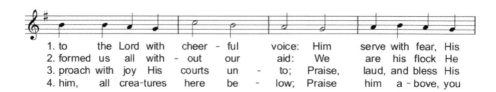
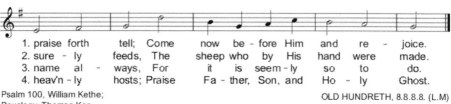

1. All people that on earth do dwell, Sing to the Lord with cheer-ful voice: Him serve with fear, His praise forth tell; Come now be-fore Him and re-joice.
2. Know that the Lord is God in - deed; He formed us all with - out our aid: We are his flock He sure - ly feeds, The sheep who by His hand were made.
3. O en - ter then His gates with praise; Ap - proach with joy His courts un - to; Praise, laud, and bless His name al - ways, For it is seem - ly so to do.
4. Praise God, from whom all bless - ings flow; Praise him, all crea-tures here be - low; Praise Fa - ther, Son, and Ho - ly Ghost.

Psalm 100, William Kethe;
Doxology, Thomas Ken.

OLD HUNDRETH, 8.8.8.8. (L.M)

10. All You Who Seek a Comfort Sure

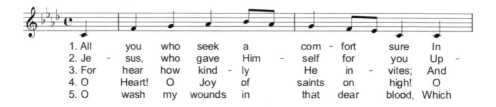

1. All you who seek a com - fort sure In trou - ble and dis - tress, What - ev - er griefs weigh
2. Je - sus, who gave Him - self for you Up - on the cross to die, O - pens to you His
3. For hear how kind - ly He in - vites; And hear His words so blest: "All you that la - bor,
4. O Heart! O Joy of saints on high! O Hope of sin - ners here! At - tract - ed by these
5. O wash my wounds in that dear blood, Which from Your pas - sion flow; New grace, new hope in -

```
1. down the      mind,    Or      guilt  the    soul   op -   press:
2. Sac-red       Heart;   O       to     that   Heart  draw   nigh!
3. come to       me,      And     I      will   give   you    rest."
4. lov-ing       words,   To      You    I      lift   my     prayer,
5. spire, a -    new      And     bet -  ter    heart  be -   stow.
```

Quicumque certum quæritis, 18th c. Latin
Tr. Edward Caswall

MORNING SONG, 8.6.8.6. (C.M.)

11

Alleluia, Alleluia

```
1. Al - le - lu - ia,    al - le - lu - ia!   Hearts to heav'n and   voic - es raise:
2. Now the    i - ron    bars are bro - ken   Christ from death to   life is born,
3. Al - le - lu - ia,    al - le - lu - ia!   Glo - ry   to   the    Fa - ther be;
```

```
1. Sing to  God  a        hymn of  glad-ness,  Sing to  God   a       hymn of praise.
2. Glo-rious life, and    life im - mor - tal, On this  ho -  ly      East - er morn.
3. Al - le - lu - ia!     to  the  Sav - ior   Who has gained the     vic - to - ry;
```

```
1. He,  who on  the       cross a   vic - tim,  For   the  world's sal - va - tion bled,
2. Christ has tri-umphed, and we    con-quer    Through his  might-y     en - ter-prise:
3. Al - le - lu - ia!     to  the   Spir - it,  Font  of   love and    sanc - ti - ty:
```

```
1. Je - sus Christ, the   King of   glo - ry    Now  is    ris - en    from the dead.
2. Hop-ing that  to       life e -  ter - nal   By   his   ris - ing   we   may rise.
3. Al - le - lu - ia,     al - le - lu - ia!    To   the   Tri - une   Maj - es - ty.
```

Christopher Wordsworth

HYMN TO JOY, 8.7.8.7. D.

12
Alleluia, Sing to Jesus

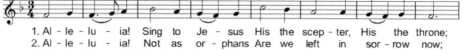

1. Alleluia! Sing to Jesus His the scepter, His the throne;
2. Alleluia! Not as orphans Are we left in sorrow now;
3. Alleluia! Bread of heaven, Here on earth our food, our stay;
4. Alleluia! King eternal, You the Lord of lords we own;

1. Alleluia! His the triumph, His the victory alone.
2. Alleluia! He is near us, Faith believes, nor questions how.
3. Alleluia! Here the sinful Flee to you from day to day.
4. Alleluia! Born of Mary, Earth your footstool, heav'n your throne.

1. Hark! The songs of peaceful Zion Thunder like a mighty flood:
2. Though the cloud from sight received him, When the forty days are o'er:
3. Intercessor, Friend of sinners, Earth's Redeemer, plead for me,
4. You within the veil have entered, Robed in flesh, our great High Priest,

1. "Jesus out of every nation Has redeemed us by his blood."
2. Shall our hearts forget His promise, "I am with you evermore"?
3. Where the songs of all the sinless Sweep across the crystal sea.
4. Here on earth both Priest and Victim In the Eucharistic feast.

William C. Dix   HYFRYDOL. 8.7.8.7. D.

13
Alma Redemptoris Mater

Alma Redemptoris Mater, quæ pervia cæli Porta manes, et stella maris,

succurre cadenti, Surgere qui curat populo: tu quæ genuisti, Natura mirante,

tuum sanctum Genitorem Virgo prius ac posterius, Gabrielis ab ore

Sumens illud Ave, peccatorum miserere.

Trad. Latin, Hermannus Contaecus   ALMA REDEMPTORIS MATER, Irregular

14

Angels We Have Heard on High

1. An - gels we have heard on high sweet - ly sing - ing
2. Shep-herds, why this ju - bi - lee? Why your joy - ous
3. Come to Beth - le - hem and see Him whose birth the
4. See him in a man - ger laid Whom the choirs of

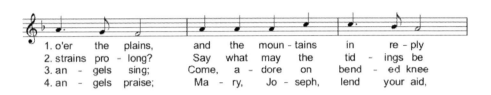

1. o'er the plains, and the moun - tains in re - ply
2. strains pro - long? Say what may the tid - ings be
3. an - gels sing; Come, a - dore on bend - ed knee
4. an - gels praise; Ma - ry, Jo - seph, lend your aid,

1. ech - o - ing their joy - ous strains.
2. Which in - spire your heav'n - ly song?
3. Christ, the Lord, the new - born King.
4. While our hears in love we raise.

Glo - - - - ri - a! in ex-cel-sis De - o!

Glo - - - ri - a! in ex-cel-sis De - o!

Les Anges dans nos campagnes, 18 c. French;
Tr. James Chadwick

GLORIA. 7.7.7.7.
with refrain

15. As with Gladness Men of Old

1. As with gladness men of old Did the guiding star behold,
As with joy they hailed its light, Leading onward, beaming bright,
So, most glorious Lord, may we Evermore be led to Thee.

2. As with joyful steps they sped To that lowly manger bed,
There to bend the knee before Him whom heav'n and earth adore;
So may we with willing feet Ever seek the mercy seat.

3. As they offered gifts most rare At that manger rude and bare;
So may we with holy joy, Pure and free from sin's alloy,
All our costliest treasures bring, Christ! to Thee, our heav'nly King.

4. Holy Jesus, ev'ry day Keep us in the narrow way;
And, when earthly things are past, Bring our ransomed souls at last
Where they need no star to guide, Where no clouds Thy glory hide.

5. In the heav'nly country bright Need they no created light;
Thou, its light, its joy, its crown, Thou its sun which goes not down;
There for ever may we sing Alleluias to our King.

William C. Dix

DIX, 7.7.7.7.7.7.

16. At the Lamb's High Feast

1. At the Lamb's high feast we sing Praise to our victorious King,
Who hath washed us in the tide

2. Where the Paschal Blood is poured, Death's dark angel sheathes his sword;
Israel's hosts triumphant go

3. Mighty Victim from on high! Hell's fierce pow'rs beneath Thee lie;
Thou has conquer'd in the fight,

4. Easter triumph, Easter joy, Sin alone can this destroy;
From sin's pow'r do Thou set free

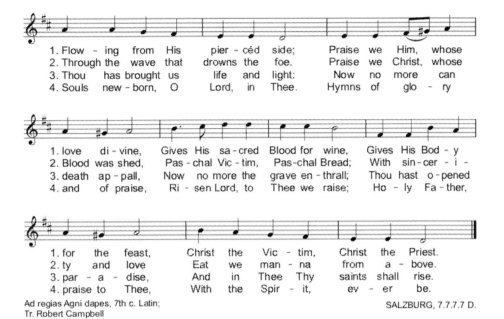

1. Flowing from His pierc-éd side; Praise we Him, whose love divine, Gives His sacred Blood for wine, Gives His Body for the feast, Christ the Victim, Christ the Priest.
2. Through the wave that drowns the foe. Praise we Christ, whose Blood was shed, Paschal Victim, Paschal Bread; With sincerity and love Eat we manna from above.
3. Thou has brought us life and light: Now no more can death appall, Now no more the grave enthrall; Thou hast opened paradise, And in Thee Thy saints shall rise.
4. Souls new-born, O Lord, in Thee. Hymns of glory and of praise, Risen Lord, to Thee we raise; Holy Father, praise to Thee, With the Spirit, ever be.

Ad regias Agni dapes, 7th c. Latin;
Tr. Robert Campbell

SALZBURG, 7.7.7.7 D.

17
Attende Domine

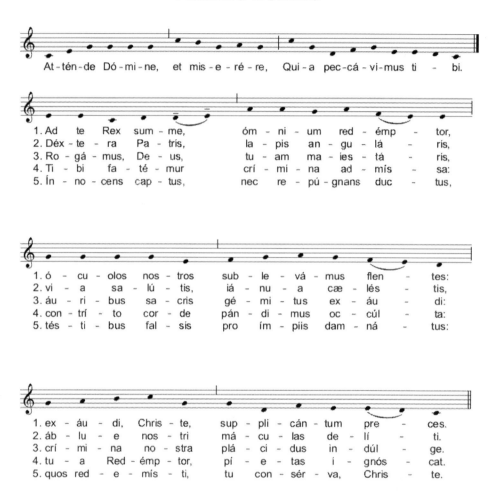

At-tén-de Dó-mi-ne, et mis-e-ré-re, Qui-a pec-cá-vi-mus ti - bi.

1. Ad te Rex sum - me, óm - ni - um red - émp - tor,
2. Déx - te - ra Pa - tris, la - pis an - gu - lá - ris,
3. Ro - gá - mus, De - us, tu - am ma - ies - tá - ris,
4. Ti - bi fa - té - mur crí - mi - na ad - mís - sa:
5. In - no - cens cap - tus, nec re - pú - gnans duc - tus,

1. ó - cu - olos nos - tros sub - le - vá - mus flen - tes:
2. vi - a sa - lú - tis, iá - nu - a cæ - lés - tis,
3. áu - ri - bus sa - cris gé - mi - tus ex - áu - di:
4. con - trí - to cor - de pán - di - mus oc - cúl - ta:
5. tés - ti - bus fal - sis pro ím - piis dam - ná - tus:

1. ex - áu - di, Chris - te, sup - pli - cán - tum pre - ces.
2. áb - lu - e nos - tri má - cu - las de - lí - ti.
3. crí - mi - na no - stra plá - ci - dus in - dúl - ge.
4. tu - a Red - émp - tor, pí - e - tas i - gnós - cat.
5. quos red - e - mís - ti, tu con - sér - va, Chris - te.

10th c. Latin

ATTENDE DOMINE, 11.11.11.
with refrain

Ave Maria

Trad. Latin. AVE MARIA, Irregular

19 Ave Regina Caelorum

A - ve, Re - gí - na cae - ló - rum, A - ve Dó - mi - na an - ge - ló - rum:
Sal - ve, ra - dix, sal - ve, por - ta Ex qua mun - do lux est or - ta:
Gau - de, Vir - go glo - ri - ó - sa, Su - per om - nes spe - ci - ó - sa,
Va - le, o val - de de - có - ra, Et pro no - bis Chris - tum e - xo - ra.

Trad. Latin. AVE REGINA CAELORUM, Irregular

20 Ave Verum Corpus (chant)

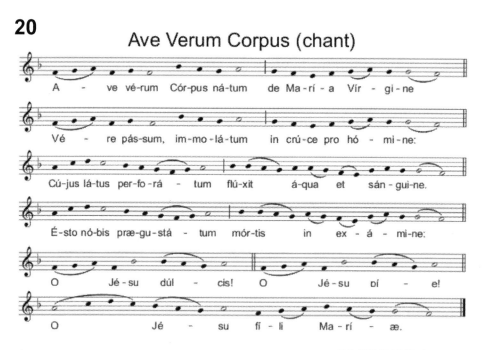

A - ve vé - rum Cór - pus ná - tum de Ma - rí - a Vír - gi - ne
Vé - re pás - sum, im - mo - lá - tum in crú - ce pro hó - mi - ne:
Cú - jus lá - tus per - fo - rá - tum flú - xit á - qua et sán - gui - ne.
É - sto nó - bis præ - gu - stá - tum mór - tis in ex - á - mi - ne:
O Jé - su dúl - cis! O Jé - su pí - e!
O Jé - su fí - li Ma - rí - æ.

14th c. Latin. AVE VERUM CORPUS, Irregular

Away in a Manger

21

1. A - way in a man - ger, no crib for a bed, The
2. The cat - tle are low - ing, the Ba - by a - wakes, But
3. Be near me, Lord Je - sus, I ask Thee to stay Close

1. lit - tle Lord Je - sus laid down His sweet head; The
2. lit - tle Lord Je - sus, no cry - ing He makes; I
3. by me for - ev - er, and love me, I pray; Bless

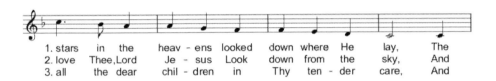
1. stars in the heav - ens looked down where He lay, The
2. love Thee, Lord Je - sus Look down from the sky, And
3. all the dear chil - dren in Thy ten - der care, And

1. lit - tle Lord Je - sus, a - sleep on the hay.
2. stay by my side un - til mom - ing is nigh.
3. fit us for heav - en to live with Thee there.

Vs 1-2 Anonymous.
Vs 3 attr. John T. McFarland

MUELLER, 11.11.11.11.

22

Be Joyful Mary

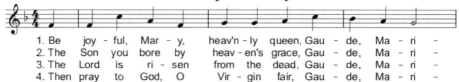

1. Be joyful, Mary, heav'nly queen, Gaude, Maria:
2. The Son you bore by heav'n's grace, Gaude, Maria:
3. The Lord is risen from the dead, Gaude, Maria:
4. Then pray to God, O Virgin fair, Gaude, Maria:

1. a: Your Son who died was living seen,
2. a: Did all our guilt and sin efface,
3. a: He rose with might as He had said,
4. a: That He our souls to heaven bear.

Alleluia, Laetare O Maria!

Regina caeli, jubila, 17th c. Latin;
Tr. Anonymous

REGINA CAELI, 8.5.8.4.7.

23

Be Still, My Soul

1. Be still, my soul: the Lord is on your side. Bear patiently the cross of grief or pain. Leave to your God to order and provide; In every change, he
2. Be still, my soul: your God does undertake To guide the future, as He has the past. Your hope, your confidence let nothing shake; All now mysterious

3. Be still, my soul: when dearest friends depart, And all is darkened in the vale of tears, Then shall you better know His love, His heart, Who comes to soothe your
4. Be still, my soul: the hour is has't'ning on When we shall be forever with the Lord. When disappointment, grief and fear are gone, Sorrow forgot, love's
5. Be still, my soul: begin the song of praise On earth, believing, to your Lord on high; Acknowledge Him in all your words and ways, So shall He view you

1. faith-ful will re - main. Be still, my soul: your best, your heav'n-ly
2. shall be bright at last. Be still, my soul: the waves and winds still
3. sor - row and your fears. Be still, my soul: your Je - sus can re-
4. pur - est joys re - stored. Be still, my soul: when change and tears are
5. with a well pleased eye. Be still, my soul: the sun of life di-

1. Friend Through thron-y ways leads to a joy - ful end.
2. know His voice who ruled them while he dwelt be - low.
3. pay From His own full - ness all He takes a - way.
4. past All safe and bless - ed we shall meet at last.
5. vine Through pass-ing clouds shall but more bright - ly shine.

Stille, meine Wille, dein Jesus hilft siegen, Kathrina von Schlegel;   FINLANDIA, 10.10.10.10.10.10.
Tr. Jane L. Borthwick

24
Be Thou My Vision

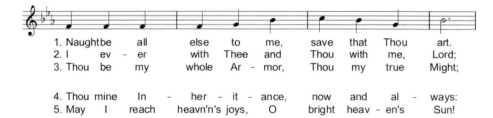

Rop tú mo baile, St. Dallán Forgaill;
Tr. Mary Byrne; Para. Eleanor Hull

SLANE, 10.10.9.10.

Beautiful Savior

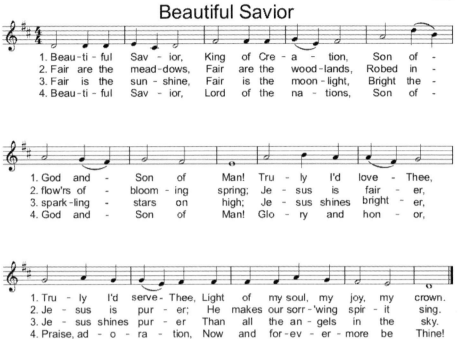

Schönster Herr Jesu
Tr. Joseph A. Seiss

CRUSADERS' HYMN 5.5.7.5.5.8.

Behold the Dwelling of God

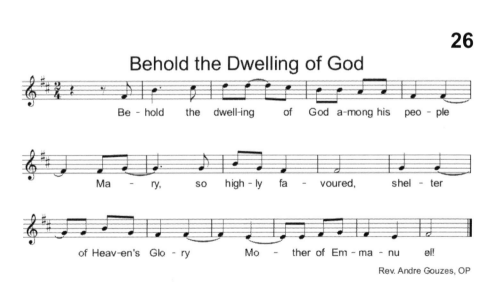

Rev. Andre Gouzes, OP

28
By the Blood that Flowed From Thee

1. By the Blood that flowed from Thee In Thy bit-ter ag-o-ny;
2. By the thorns that crowned Thy Head; By Thy scep-tre of a reed;
3. By the nails and point-ed spear; By Thy peop-le's cruel jeer;
4. By the dark-ness thick as night Blot-ting out the sun from sight;
5. By Thy weep-ing Moth-er's woe; By the sword that pierced her through,

1. By the scourge so meek-ly borne; By Thy pur-ple
2. By Thy Foot-steps faint and slow, Weighed be-neath Thy
3. By Thy dy-ing prayer which rose Beg-ging mer-cy
4. By the cry with which in death Thou did yield Thy
5. When, in an-guish stand-ing by, On the Cross she

1. robe of scorn
2. Cross of woe,
3. for Thy foes. Je-sus Sav-ior hear our cry! Thou went suff'-ring
4. part-ing Breath.
5. saw Thee die.

once as we; Hear the lov-ing li-ta-ny We Thy chil-dren sing to Thee.

Frederick W. Faber; Cecilia M. Caddell

TICHFIELD 7.7.7.7. D.

29. Christ the Lord is Risen Today

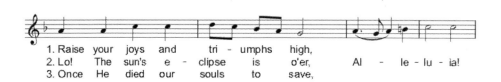

Surexit Christus hodie, 14th c. Latin
Tr. Charles Wesley

LLANFAIR, 7.7.7.7
with Alleluias

30. Christus Vincit

Trad. Latin

CHRISTUS VINCIT, 8.8.

Come Down, O Love Divine

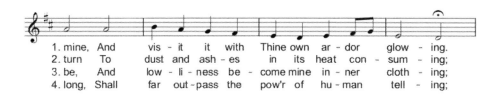

1. Come down, O Love di-vine, seek Thou this soul of
2. O let it free-ly burn, till earth-ly pas-sions
3. Let ho-ly char-i-ty mine out-ward ves-ture
4. And so the yearn-ing strong, with which the soul will

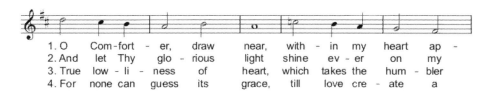

1. mine, And vis-it it with Thine own ar-dor glow-ing.
2. turn To dust and ash-es in its heat con-sum-ing;
3. be, And low-li-ness be-come mine in-ner cloth-ing;
4. long, Shall far out-pass the pow'r of hu-man tell-ing;

1. O Com-fort-er, draw near, with-in my heart ap-
2. And let Thy glo-rious light shine ev-er on my
3. True low-li-ness of heart, which takes the hum-bler
4. For none can guess its grace, till love cre-ate a

1. pear, And kin-dle it, Thy ho-ly flame be-stow-ing.
2. sight, And clothe me round, the while my path il-lum-ing.
3. part, And o'er its own short-com-ings weeps with loath-ing.
4. place Where-in the Ho-ly Spir-it makes a dwell-ing.

Discendi, Amor santo, Bianco da Siena;
Tr. Richard F. Littledale

DOWN AMPNEY, 6.6.11. D.

32
Come, Holy Ghost

1. Come, Holy Ghost, Creator blest, And in our hearts take up Thy rest; Come with Thy grace and heav'nly aid To fill the hearts which Thou has made, To fill the hearts which Thou hast made.
2. O Comforter, to Thee we cry, Thou heav'nly gift of God most high; Thou fount of life, and fire of love, And sweet anointing from above, And sweet anointing from above.
3. O Holy Ghost, through Thee alone, Know we the Father and the Son; Be this our firm unchanging creed, That Thou dost from Them both proceed, That thou dost from Them both proceed.
4. Praise we the Lord, Father and Son, And Holy Spirit with Them one; And may the Son on us bestow All gifts that from the Spirit flow, All gifts that from the Spirit flow.

Veni Creator Spiritus, Rabanus Maurus;
Tr. Edward Caswall

LAMBILLOTTE, 8.8.8.8. LM.
with refrain

33
Come, My Way, My Truth, My Life

1. Come, my Way, my Truth, my Life: Such a way as gives us breath; Such a truth as ends all strife, Such a
2. Come, my Light, my Feast, my Strength: Such a light as shows a feast, Such a feast as mends in length, Such a
3. Come, my Joy, my Love, my Heart: Such a joy as none can move, Such a love as none can part, Such a

	1. life	as	kill				eth	death.
	2. strength	as	makes				his	guest.
	3. heart	as	joys				in	love.

George Herbert

THE CALL, 7.7.7.7.

34

Come, Thou Almighty King

1. Come, Thou al - might - y King, Help us Thy Name to
2. Come, Thou in - car - nate Word, Gird on Thy might - y
3. Come, ho - ly Com - fort - er, Thy sa - cred wit - ness

1. sing: Help us to praise: Fa - ther all glo - ri - ous, Ev - er vic -
2. sword; Our prayer at - tend. Come and Thy peo - ple bless, And give Thy
3. bear in this glad hour! Thou, Who al - might - y art, Now rule in

1. to - ri - ous, Come and reign o - ver us, An - cient of Days.
2. Word suc-cess, And let Thy right - eous-ness On us de - scend.
3. ev - 'ry heart, Ne - ver from us de - part, Spir - it of pow'r.

Attr. Charles Wesley

ITALIAN HYMN, 6.6.4.6.6.6.4.

35

Come, Thou Long-Expected Jesus

1. Come, Thou long ex - pect-ed Je - sus, Born to set Thy peo - ple free;
2. Is - rael's strength and con-so - la - tion, Hope of all the earth Thou art;
3. Born Thy peo - ple to de - liv - er, Born a child and yet a King,
4. By Thine own e - ter - nal Spir - it Rule in all our hearts a - lone;

1. From our fears and sins re - lease us, Let us find our rest in Thee.
2. Dear de - sire of ev - 'ry na - tion, Joy of ev - 'ry long - ing heart.
3. Born to reign in us for ev - er Now Thy gra - cious king-dom bring.
4. By the son-ship we in - her - it, Raise us to Thy glo-rious throne.

Charles Wesley

STUTTGART, 8.7.8.7.

36
Comfort, Comfort, O My People

1. Com-fort, com-fort, O my peo-ple, Speak of peace, Thus says our God;
2. For the her-ald's voice is cry-ing In the de-sert far and near,
3. Yea, her sins our God will par-don, Blot-ting out each dark mis-deed;
4. Straight-en that which long was crook-ed, Make the rough-er plac-es plain:

1. Com-fort those who sit in dark-ness, Mourn-ing 'neath their sor-row's load;
2. Bid-ding all men to re-pent-ance, Since the king-dom now is here.
3. All that well de-served His an-ger He will no more see nor heed.
4. Let your hearts be true and hum-ble, As be-fits His ho-ly reign,

1. Speak un-to Je-ru-sa-lem Of the peace that waits for them;
2. O that warn-ing cry o-bey! Now pre-pare for God a way!
3. She has suf-fered man-y'a day, Now her griefs have passed a-way,
4. For the glo-ry of the Lord Now o'er earth is shed a-broad,

1. Tell her that her sins I cov-er, And her war-fare now is o-ver.
2. Let the val-leys rise to meet Him, And the hills bow down to greet Him.
3. God will change her pin-ing sad-ness In-to ev-er spring-ing glad-ness.
4. And all flesh shall see the to-ken That His word is nev-er bro-ken.

Tröstet, tröstet meine Lieven, Johann Olearius;
Tr. Catherine Winkworth

GENEVAN 42, 8.7.8.7.7.7.8.8.

Creator of the Stars of Night

1. Cre - a - tor of the stars of night,
2. In pit - y lest the an - cient curse
3. You came the Bride - groom of the bride,

4. At whose high name, ma - jes - tic now,
5. O Thou whose co - ming is with dread
6. To God the Fa - ther, God the Son,

1. Your peo - ple's ev - er - last - ing light,
2. Should doom to death a u - ni - verse,
3. As drew the world to eve - ning - tide;

4. All knees must bend, all hearts must bow:
5. To judge the liv - ing and the dead,
6. And God the Spir - it, Three in One,

1. O Christ, Re - deem - er, save us all,
2. O Lord, you came in truth and grace
3. Pro - ceed - ing from a vir - gin shrine,

4. All things in heav'n, all things be - low
5. Pre serve us, while we dwell be low
6. Laud, ho - nor, might, and glo - ry be

1. And hear Your ser - vants when they call.
2. To save and heal a ru - ined race.
3. The spot - less Vic - tim all di - vine.

4. Shall call You Lord and God a - lone.
5. From ev 'ry in - sult of the foe.
6. From age to age e - ter - nal - ly. A - men.

Conditor Alme Siderum, 7th c. Latin
Tr. John M. Neale, alt

CONDITOR ALME SIDERUM, 8.8.8.8. (L.M)

38
Crown Him With Many Crowns

1. Crown Him with many crowns, The Lamb upon His throne; Hark!
2. Crown Him the Lord of love, Behold His hands and side, Rich
3. Crown Him the Son of God Before the worlds began, And

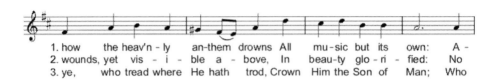

1. how the heav'nly anthem drowns All music but its own: A-
2. wounds, yet visible above, In beauty glorified: No
3. ye, who tread where He hath trod, Crown Him the Son of Man; Who

1. wake, my soul, and sing Of Him who died for thee, And
2. angel in the sky Can fully bear the sight, But
3. every grief hath known That wrings the human breast, And

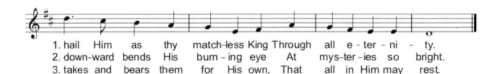

1. hail Him as thy matchless King Through all eternity.
2. downward bends His burning eye At mysteries so bright.
3. takes and bears them for His own, That all in Him may rest.

Vs. 1, 3 Matthew Bridges
Vs. 2 Godfrey Thring

DIADEMATA, 6.6.8.6. (S.M) D.

Daily, Daily Sing to Mary

1. Daily, Daily sing to Mary; Sing, my soul, her praises due.
2. She is mighty to deliver; Call her, trust her lovingly.
3. Sing, my tongue, the Virgin's honors, Who for us her Maker bore.

1. All her glorious actions cherish, With the heart's devotion true.
2. When the tempest rages 'round you, She will calm the troubled sea.
3. For the curse of old inflicted, Peace and blessings to restore.

1. Lost in wond'ring contemplation, Be her majesty confessed!
2. Gifts of heaven she has given, Noble Lady, to our race;
3. Sing in songs of praise unending, Sing the world's majestic Queen;

1. Call her Mother, call her Virgin, Happy Mother, Virgin blest!
2. She, the Queen who clothes her subjects With the light of God's own grace.
3. Weary not nor faint in telling All the gifts that earth has seen.

St. Casimir;
Tr. Henry Bittleston

ALLE TAGE SING UNID SAGE, 8.7.8.7. D.

40
Draw Near and Take the Body of the Lord

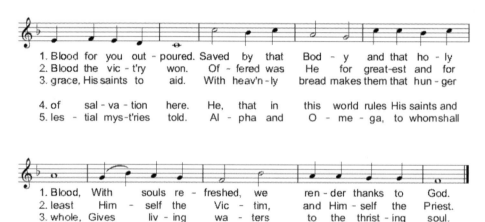

1. Draw near and take the Body of the Lord, And drink the holy Blood for you out-poured. Saved by that Body and that holy Blood, With souls refreshed, we render thanks to God.
2. Salvation's giver, Christ, God's only Son, By His dear Cross and Blood the vict'ry won. Offered was He for greatest and for least Himself the Victim, and Himself the Priest.
3. He, Ransomer from death, and Light from shade Now gives His holy grace, His saints to aid. With heav'nly bread makes them that hunger whole, Gives living waters to the thristing soul.
4. Let us approach with faithful hearts sincere, And take the pledges of salvation here. He, that in this world rules His saints and shields, To all believers life eternal yields.
5. Victims were offered by the law of old, That in a type celestial myst'ries told. Alpha and Omega, to whom shall bow All nations at the doom, is with us now.

Sancti venite, corpus Christi sumite
Tr. J. M. Neale

ANIMA CHRISTE (MAHER), 10.10.10.10.

41
Drop, Drop Slow Tears

1. Drop, drop, slow tears, and bathe those beauteous feet, Which brought from heav'n the news and Prince of peace.
2. Cease not, wet eyes, His mercies to entreat; To cry for vengeance tho' sin never cease.
3. In your deep floods drown all my faults and fears; Nor let His eye see sin, but through my tears.

Phineas Fletcher

SONG 46, 10.10.

42

Faith of Our Fathers

1. Faith of our fathers, living still, In spite of
2. Faith of our fathers, we will strive To win all
3. Faith of our fathers, we will love Both friend and

1. dungeon, fire and sword; O how our hearts beat
2. nations unto thee; And through the truth that
3. foe in all our strife; And preach thee, too, as

1. high with joy When-e'er we hear that glorious Word.
2. comes from God, We all shall then be truly free.
3. love knows how By kindly words and virtuous life.

Faith of our fathers, holy faith! We will be true to thee till death.

Frederick Faber   ST. CATHERINE, 8.8.8.8.8.8.

43. Faithful Cross

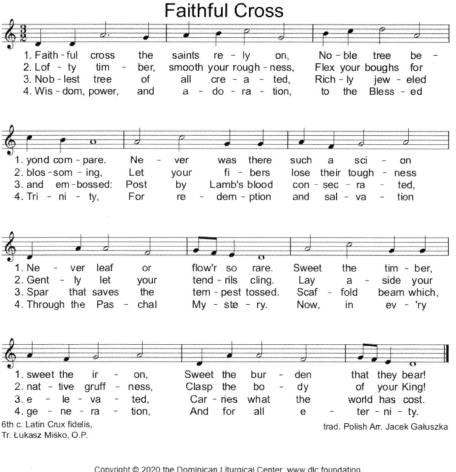

1. Faithful cross the saints rely on, Noble tree beyond compare. Never was there such a scion Never leaf or flow'r so rare. Sweet the timber, sweet the iron,
2. Lofty timber, smooth your roughness, Flex your boughs for blossoming, Let your fibers lose their toughness Gently let your tendrils cling. Lay aside your native gruffness, Clasp the body
3. Noblest tree of all created, Richly jeweled and embossed: Post by Lamb's blood consecrated, Spar that saves the tempest tossed. Scaffold beam which elevated, Carries what the world has cost.
4. Wisdom, power, and adoration, to the Blessed Trinity, For redemption and salvation Through the Paschal Mystery. Now, in ev'ry generation, And for all eternity.

6th c. Latin Crux fidelis,
Tr. Łukasz Miśko, O.P.

trad. Polish Arr. Jacek Gałuszka

Copyright © 2020 the Dominican Liturgical Center: www.dlc.foundation

44. Firmly I Believe and Truly

1. Firmly I believe, and truly, God is Three, and
2. And I trust and hope most fully In that Manhood
3. Simply to His grace and wholly Light and life and

4. And I hold in veneration, For the love of
5. And I take with joy whatever Now besets me,
6. Adoration aye be given, With and through the'an-

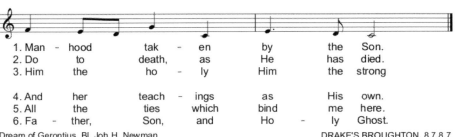

Dream of Gerontius, Bl. Joh H. Newman   DRAKE'S BROUGHTON, 8.7.8.7.

45

For All the Saints

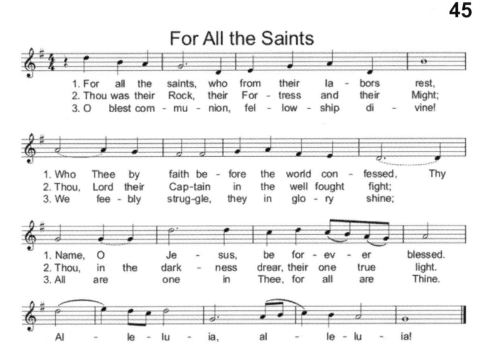

William Walsham How.   SINE NOMINE, 10.10.10.
with Alleluias

46
For the Beauty of the Earth

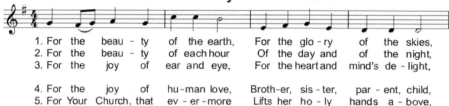

1. For the beau-ty of the earth, For the glo-ry of the skies,
2. For the beau-ty of each hour Of the day and of the night,
3. For the joy of ear and eye, For the heart and mind's de-light,
4. For the joy of hu-man love, Broth-er, sis-ter, par-ent, child,
5. For Your Church, that ev-er-more Lifts her ho-ly hands a-bove,
6. For each per-fect gift sub-lime To our race so free-ly giv'n,

1. For the love which from our birth O-ver and a-round us lies.
2. Hill and vale, and tree and flow'r, Sun and moon, and stars of light.
3. For the mys-tic har-mo-ny Link-ing sense to sound and sight.
4. Friends on earth and friends a-bove, For all gen-tle thoughts and mild.
5. Of-fring up on eve-ry shore Her pure sac-ri-fice of love.
6. Grac-es hu-man and di-vine, Flow'rs of earth and buds of heav'n.

Christ, our Lord, to You we raise This our hymn of grate-ful praise.

Folliot S. Pierpoint   DIX, 7.7.7.7.7.7.

47
Forty Days and Forty Nights

1. For-ty days and for-ty nights You were fast-ing in the wild;
2. Shall not we Your sor-row share And from earth-ly joys ab-stain,
3. And if Sa-tan armed for war, Flesh or spir-it should as-sail,

1. For-ty days and for-ty nights Tempt-ed, and yet un-de-filed.
2. Fast-ing with un-ceas-ing prayer, Glad with You to suf-fer pain?
3. You his Van-quish-er be-fore, Grant we may not faint or fail.

George H. Smyttan   HEINLEIN, 7.7.7.7.

48
From All that Dwell Below the Skies

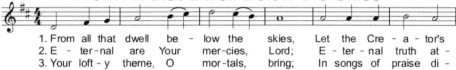

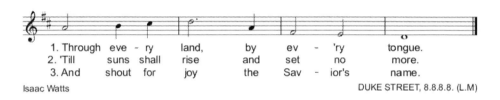

1. From all that dwell be - low the skies, Let the Cre - a - tor's praise a - rise; Let the Re - deem-er's name be sung, Through eve - ry land, by ev - 'ry tongue.
2. E - ter - nal are Your mer-cies, Lord; E - ter - nal truth at - tends Your word: Your praise shall sound from shore to shore, 'Till suns shall rise and set no more.
3. Your loft - y theme, O mor-tals, bring; In songs of praise di - vine - ly sing; The great sal - va - tion loud pro - claim, And shout for joy the Sav - ior's name.

Isaac Watts

DUKE STREET, 8.8.8.8. (L.M)

49
God is Love, Let Heaven Adore Him

1. God is Love: let heav'n a - dore Him; God is Love: let earth re - joice; Let cre - a - tion sing be - fore Him, And ex - alt Him with one voice. He who laid the earth's foun - da - tion, He who spread the heav'ns a - bove, He who breathes through all cre - a - tion, He is Love, e - ter - nal Love.

2. God is Love: and He en - fold - eth All the world in one em - brace; With un - fail - ing grasp He hold - eth Ev - 'ry child of eve - ry race. And when hu - man hearts are break - ing Un - der sor - row's i - ron rod, Then they find that self - same ach - ing Deep with - in the heart of God.

3. God is Love: and though With blind - ness Sin af - flicts the souls of men, God's e - ter - nal lov - ing kind - ness Holds and guides them e - ven then. Sin and death and hell shall nev - er O'er us fi - nal tri - umph gain; God is Love, so Love for ev - er O'er the u - ni - verse must reign.

Timothy Rees HYFRYDOL, 8.7.8.7 D.

50

God, Whose Almighty Word

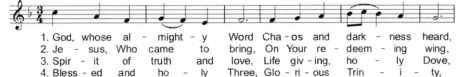

1. God, whose al - might - y Word Cha - os and dark - ness heard,
2. Je - sus, Who came to bring, On Your re - deem - ing wing,
3. Spir - it of truth and love, Life giv - ing, ho - ly Dove,
4. Bless - ed and ho - ly Three, Glo - ri - ous Trin - i - ty,

1. And took their flight; Hear us, we hum - bly pray, And where the
2. Heal - ing and sight, Health to the sick in mind, Sight to the
3. Speed forth Your flight; Move on the wa - ter's face, Bear - ing the
4. Wis - dom, love, might! Bound-less as o - cean's tide, Roll - ing in

1. Gos - pel's day Sheds not its glo - rious ray, Let there be light!
2. in - ly blind: Oh, now to all man - kind Let there be light!
3. lamp of grace, And, in earth's dark - est place, Let there be light!
4. full - est pride, Through the world, far and wide, Let there be light!

John Marriott   ITALIAN HYMN, 6.6.4.6.6.6.4.

51
Godhead Here in Hiding

1. Godhead here in hiding whom I do adore, Masked by these bare shadows, shape and nothing more, See, Lord, at Thy service low lies here a heart Lost, all lost in wonder at the God Thou art.
2. Seeing, touching, tasting are in Thee deceived: How says trusty hearing? that shall be believed; What God's Son has told me, take for truth I do; Truth himself speaks truly or there's nothing true.
3. On the cross Thy Godhead made no sign to men, Here Thy very manhood steals from human ken: Both are my confession, both are my belief, and I pray the prayer of the dying thief.
4. I am not like Thomas, wounds I cannot see, But can plainly call Thee Lord and God as he; This faith each day deeper be my holding of, Daily make me harder hope and dearer love.
5. O Thou our reminder of Christ crucified, Living Bread, the life of us for whom He died, Lend this life to me then: feed and feast my mind, There be Thou the sweetness man was meant to find.
6. Bring the tender tale true of the Pelican; Bathe me, Jesus Lord, in what Thy bosom ran — Blood whereof a single drop has pow'r to win All the world forgiveness of its world of sin.
7. Jesus, Whom I look at shrouded here below, I beseech thee send me what I thirst for so, Some day to gaze on Thee face to face in light And be blest forever with thy glory's sight. Amen.

Adoro te devote, St. Thomas Aquinas;
Tr. Gerard M. Hopkins, S.J.

ADORO TE DEVOTE 11.11.11.11.

52

Guide Me, O Thou Great Redeemer

1. Guide me, O Thou great Re-deem-er Pil-grim through this
2. O-pen now the crys-tal foun-tain Whence the heal-ing
3. When I tread the verge of Jor-dan, Bid my anx-ious

1. bar-ren Land, I am weak, but Thou art might-y, Hold me with Thy
2. streams do flow, Let the fier-y cloud-y pil-lar Lead me all my
3. fear sub-side; Death of deaths, and hell's de-struc-tion, Land me safe on

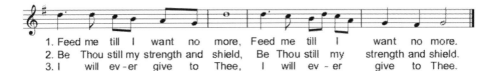

1. pow'r-ful Hand; Bread of heav-en, Bread of heav-en,
2. jour-ney through; Strong De-liv'r-er, strong De-liv'r-er
3. Can-aan's side. Songs of prais-es, songs of prais-es,

1. Feed me till I want no more, Feed me till I want no more.
2. Be Thou still my strength and shield, Be Thou still my strength and shield.
3. I will ev-er give to Thee, I will ev-er give to Thee.

William Williams
Tr. Peter Williams

CWM RHONDDA 8.7.8.7.8.7.7.

53. Hail, O Bright Star of Ocean

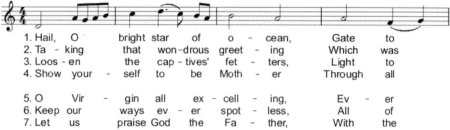

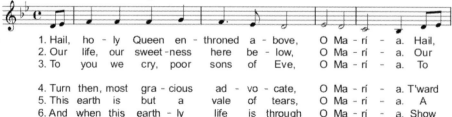

1. Hail, O bright star of ocean, Gate to that joy supernal, Blest ever-virgin, Mother of our high God eternal!
2. Taking that wondrous greeting Which was by Gabriel spoken, Changing "Eva" to "Ave," Be of God's peace the token.
3. Loosen the captives' fetters, Light to the blind restoring, All of our wrongs dispelling, All that is good imploring.
4. Show yourself to be Mother Through all your supplication. He, then, will hear, who chose you At His blest Incarnation.
5. O Virgin all excelling, Ever mild, meek, and lowly, Freed from all sin, preserve us, Make us pure, chaste, and holy.
6. Keep our ways ever spotless, All of our ways defending, Till we shall gaze on Jesus With bliss-ful joy unending.
7. Let us praise God the Father, With the Son's worship blending, And with the Holy Spirit, In one great praise unending.

Ave maris stella, tr. cento Arr. Dawid Kusz, O.P. Kancjonały staniąteckie

Copyright © 2020 the Dominican Liturgical Center: www.dlc.foundation

54. Hail, Holy Queen Enthroned Above

1. Hail, holy Queen enthroned above, O María. Hail,
2. Our life, our sweetness here below, O María. Our
3. To you we cry, poor sons of Eve, O María. To
4. Turn then, most gracious advocate, O María. T'ward
5. This earth is but a vale of tears, O María. A
6. And when this earthly life is through, O María. Show
7. O gentle, gracious Mother sweet, O María. O

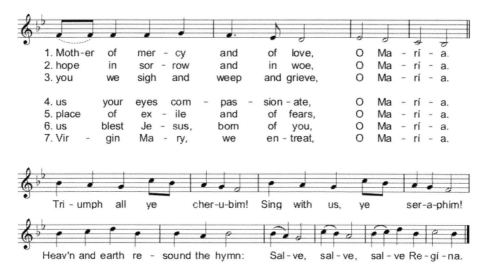

1. Mother of mercy and of love, O María.
2. hope in sorrow and in woe, O María.
3. you we sigh and weep and grieve, O María.
4. us your eyes compassionate, O María.
5. place of exile and of fears, O María.
6. us blest Jesus, born of you, O María.
7. Virgin Mary, we entreat, O María.

Triumph all ye cherubim! Sing with us, ye seraphim!
Heav'n and earth resound the hymn: Salve, salve, salve Regína.

Salve Regina, Hermannus Contraecuse;
Tr. *Roman Hymnal* atr

SALVE REGINA COELITUM, 8.4.8.4.7.7.7.9.

55

Hail the Day That Sees Him Rise

1. Hail the day that sees Him rise,
2. There the glorious triumph waits, Alleluia!
3. See Thy faithful servants, see,

1. To His throne above the skies,
2. Lift your heads, eternal gates, Alleluia!
3. Ever gazing up to Thee,

1. Christ, awhile to mortals giv'n,
2. Christ has conquered death and sin, Alleluia!
3. Circled round with angel pow'rs

1. Reascends His native heav'n,
2. Reascends His native heav'n, Alleluia!
3. Their triumphant Lord, and ours,

Charles Wesley

LLANFAIR 7.7.7.7

56. Hark! A Thrilling Voice is Calling

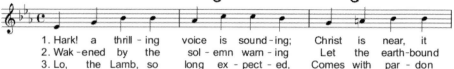

1. Hark! a thrill-ing voice is sound-ing; Christ is near, it seems to say, Cast a-way the works of dark-ness, O you chil-dren of the day.
2. Wak-ened by the sol-emn warn-ing Let the earth-bound soul a-rise; Christ, her Sun, all ill dis-pel-ling, Shines up-on the morn-ing skies.
3. Lo, the Lamb, so long ex-pect-ed, Comes with par-don down from heav'n; Let us haste, with tears of sor-row, One and all to be for-giv'n.

Latin, 5th century
Tr. Edward Caswall

MERTON 8.7.8.7.

57. Hark! The Herald Angels Sing

1. Hark! The her-ald an-gels sing: "Glo-ry to the new-born King! Peace on earth, and mer-cy mild: God and sin-ners rec-on-ciled!" Joy-ful, all ye na-tions, rise; Join the tri-umph of the skies;
2. Christ, by high-est heav'n a-dored, Christ, the ev-er-last-ing Lord, Late in time, be-hold Him come: Off-spring of the Vir-gin's womb. Veiled in flesh, the God-head see. Hail, the'in-car-nate De-i-ty,
3. Hail, the heav'n-born Prince of peace! Hail, the Sun of right-eous-ness! Light and life to all He brings, Ris'n with heal-ing in His wings. Mild, He lays His glo-ry by, Born that man no more may die,

1. With the'an-gel-ic host pro-claim: "Christ is born in Beth-le-hem!"
2. Pleased as man with men to dwell: Je-sus, our E-ma-nu-el!
3. Born to raise the sons of earth; Born to give them sec-ond birth.

Hark! the her-ald an-gels sing: "Glo-ry to the new-born King!"

Hark! how all the welkin rings, Charles Wesley
Alt. George Whitefield

MENDELSSOHN 7.7.7.7. D.
with refrain

58

Hear Us O Mighty Lord

Hear us, O migh-ty Lord, show us your Mer-cy: Sin-ners we stand be-fore You.

1. To Thee, Re-deem-er on Thy throne of glo-ry:
2. O Thou chief cor-ner-stone, right hand of the Fa-ther:
3. God, we im-plore Thee, in Thy glo-ry sea-ted
4. Sins oft com-mit-ted now we lay be-fore Thee:
5. In-no-cent, cap-tive, tak-en un-re-sis-ting:

1. lift we our weep-ing eyes in ho-ly ar-dent plead-ings:
2. way of sal-va-tion, gate of life ce-le-stial:
3. bow down and hear-ken to Thy weep-ing chil-dren:
4. with true con-tri-tion, now no more we veil them:
5. false-ly ac-cus-ed and for us sin-ners sen-tenced,

1. lis-ten O Je-sus, to our sup-pli-ca-tions.
2. cleanse our sin-ful souls from all de-file-ment.
3. pi-ty and par-don all our grie-vious tres-pass-es.
4. grant us Re-deem-er, lov-ing ab-so-lu-tion.
5. save us, we pray Thee, Je-sus our Re-dee-mer.

10th c. Latin
Tr. W.J. Birkbeck

ATTENDE DOMINE, 11.11.11.
with refrain

59

Holy, Holy, Holy

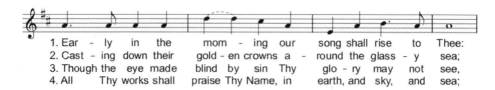

1. Holy, Holy, Holy! Lord God Almighty! Early in the morning our song shall rise to Thee; Holy, Holy, Holy! Merciful and mighty, God in three Persons, blessed Trinity.
2. Holy, Holy, Holy! All the saints adore Thee, Casting down their golden crowns around the glassy sea; Cherubim and seraphim falling down before Thee, Who was, and is, and evermore shall be.
3. Holy, Holy, Holy! Though the darkness hide Thee, Though the eye made blind by sin Thy glory may not see, Only thou art Holy; there is none beside Thee, Perfect in pow'r, in love, and purity.
4. Holy, Holy, Holy! Lord God Almighty! All Thy works shall praise Thy Name, in earth, and sky, and sea; Holy, Holy, Holy! Merciful and mighty, God in three Persons, blessed Trinity.

Reginald Heber   NICAEA, 11.12.12.10.

60

Holy God, We Praise Thy Name

1. Holy God, we praise Thy name; Lord of all, we bow before Thee.
2. Hark! the loud celestial hymn Angel choirs above are raising;
3. Holy Father, Holy Son, Holy Spirit Three we name Thee;

1. All on earth Thy scep-ter claim, All in heav'n a-bove a-dore Thee.
2. Cher-u-bim and Ser-a-phim, In un-ceas-ing chor-us prais-ing,
3. While in es-sence on-ly one, Un-di-vid-ed God we claim Thee,

1. In-fi-nite Thy vast do-main, Ev-er-last-ing is Thy reign.
2. Fill the heav'ns with sweet ac-cord: "Ho-ly, ho-ly, ho-ly Lord!"
3. And a-dor-ing bend the knee, While we own the mys-ter-y.

Grosser Gott, wirloben Dich (Te Deum), Ignax Franz;
Tr. Clarence Walworth

GROSSER GOTT, 7.8.7.8.7.7.

61

Holy Patron, Thee Saluting

1. Ho-ly pa-tron, thee sa-lut-ing Here we meet, with
2. World-ly dan-gers for them fear-ing, Youth-ful hearts to
3. Thou who faith-ful-ly at-tend-ed Him whom heav'n and
4. May our fer-vent pray'rs as-cend-ing Move thee for our

1. hearts sin-cere; Blest Saint Jo-seph, all u-nit-ing, Call on thee to
2. thee we bring, Grant, in vir-tue per-se-ver-ing, Vice may ne'er their
3. earth a-dore; Who with pi-ous care de-fend-ed Mar-y, Vir-gin
4. souls to plead; May thy smile of peace de-scend-ing, Ben-e-dic-tions

1. hear our prayer.
2. bos-om sting.
3. ev-er pure. Hap-py Saint, in bliss a-dor-ing Je-sus, Sav-ior of man-kind,
4. on us shed.

Hear thy chil-dren thee im-plor-ing, May we thy pro-tec-tion find.

Rev. P. J. Nicholas

PLEADING SAVIOR, 8.7.8.7 D.

62
How Firm a Foundation

1. How firm a foun-da-tion, you saints of the Lord, Is
2. In ev-'ry con-di-tion, in sick-ness, in health, In
3. "Fear not, I am with you, O be not dis-mayed, For

1. laid for your faith in His ex-cel-lent word! What
2. pov-er-ty's vale, or a-bound-ing in wealth; At
3. I am your God, and will still give you aid; I'll

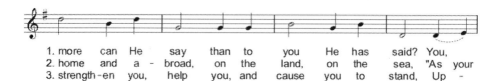
1. more can He say than to you He has said? You,
2. home and a-broad, on the land, on the sea, "As your
3. strength-en you, help you, and cause you to stand, Up -

1. who un-to Je-sus for ref-uge have fled.
2. days may de-mand, shall your strength ev-er be."
3. held by my right-eous om-ni-po-tent hand."

George Keith and R. Keen   FOUNDATION, 11.11.11.11.

63
I Heard the Voice of Jesus Say

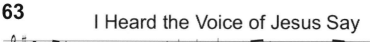

1. I heard the voice of Je-sus say, "Come un-to me and rest; Lay
2. I heard the voice of Je-sus say, "Be-hold, I free-ly give The
3. I heard the voice of Je-sus say, "I am this dark world's light; Look

1. down, thou wea-ry one, lay down thy head up-on My breast." I
2. liv-ing wa-ter; thirst-y one, Stoop down, and drink, and live." I
3. un-to me, thy morn shall rise, And all thy day be bright." I

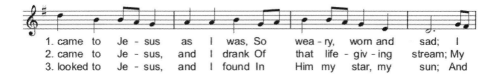

1. came to Jesus as I was, So weary, worn and sad; I
2. came to Jesus, and I drank Of that life-giving stream; My
3. looked to Jesus, and I found In Him my star, my sun; And

1. found in Him a resting place, And He has made me glad.
2. thirst was quenched, my soul revived, And now I live in Him.
3. in that light of life I'll walk Till trav-'ling days are done.

Horatius Bonar

KINGSFOLD 8.6.8.6. (C.M) D.

64

I Know that My Redeemer Lives

1. I know that my Redeemer lives; What joy the
2. He lives to bless me with His love, He lives to
3. He lives triumphant from the grave, He lives e-
4. He lives to silence all my fears, He lives to
5. He lives and grants me daily breath; He lives, and
6. He lives, all glory to His name! He lives, my

1. blest assurance gives! He lives, He lives, Who
2. plead for me above. He lives my hungry
3. ternally to save, He lives all glorious
4. wipe away my tears. He lives, and while He
5. I shall conquer death: He lives, my mansion
6. Jesus, still the same. What joy this blest as-

1. once was dead; He lives, my ever living Head.
2. soul to feed, He lives to help in time of need.
3. in the sky, He lives exalted there on high.
4. lives, I'll sing; He lives, my Prophet, Priest, and King.
5. to prepare; He lives to bring me safely there.
6. surance gives: I know that my Redeemer lives!

Samuel Medley

DUKE STREET 8.8.8.8. (L.M)

65 I Sing the Mighty Power of God

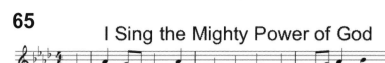

1. I sing the might-y pow'r of God That made the moun-tains rise, That
2. I sing the good-ness of the Lord That filled the earth with food; He

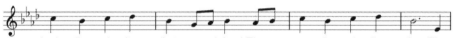

1. spread the flow-ing seas a-broad, And built the loft-y skies, I
2. formed the crea-tures with His Word And then pro-nounced them good. Lord,

1. sing the wis-dom that or-dained The sun to rule the day; The
2. how Thy won-ders are dis-played Where-e'er I turn my eye: If

1. moon shines full at His com-mand And all the stars o-bey.
2. I sur-vey the ground I tread Or gaze up-on the sky!

Isaac Watts   ELLACOMBE 8.6.8.6. (C.M) D.

66 Immaculate Mary

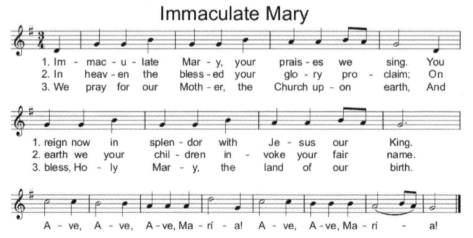

1. Im-mac-u-late Mar-y, your prais-es we sing. You
2. In heav-en the bless-ed your glo-ry pro-claim; On
3. We pray for our Moth-er, the Church up-on earth, And

1. reign now in splen-dor with Je-sus our King.
2. earth we your chil-dren in-voke your fair name.
3. bless, Ho-ly Mar-y, the land of our birth.

A-ve, A-ve, A-ve, Ma-rí-a! A-ve, A-ve, Ma-rí-a!

Lourdes Hymn, Abbe Gaignet;   LOURDES HYMN 11.11.
Tr. Jeremiah Cummings   with refrain

Immortal, Invisible, God Only Wise

67

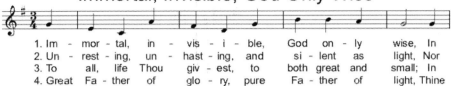

1. Im-mor-tal, in-vis-i-ble, God on-ly wise, In
2. Un-rest-ing, un-hast-ing, and si-lent as light, Nor
3. To all, life Thou giv-est, to both great and small; In
4. Great Fa-ther of glo-ry, pure Fa-ther of light, Thine

1. light in-ac-ces-si-ble hid from our eyes, Most
2. want-ing nor wast-ing, Thou rul-est in might; Thy
3. all life Thou liv-est, the true life of all; We
4. an-gels a-dore Thee, all veil-ing their sight; All

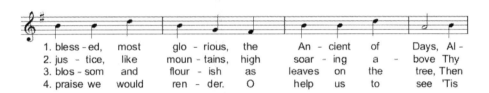

1. bless-ed, most glo-rious, the An-cient of Days, Al-
2. jus-tice, like moun-tains, high soar-ing a-bove Thy
3. blos-som and flour-ish as leaves on the tree, Then
4. praise we would ren-der. O help us to see 'Tis

1. might-y, vic-to-rious, Thy great name we praise.
2. clouds, which are foun-tains of good-ness and love.
3. with-er and per-ish, but naught chang-eth Thee.
4. on-ly the splen-dor of light hid-eth Thee.

Walter C. Smith   ST. DENIO 11.11.11.11.

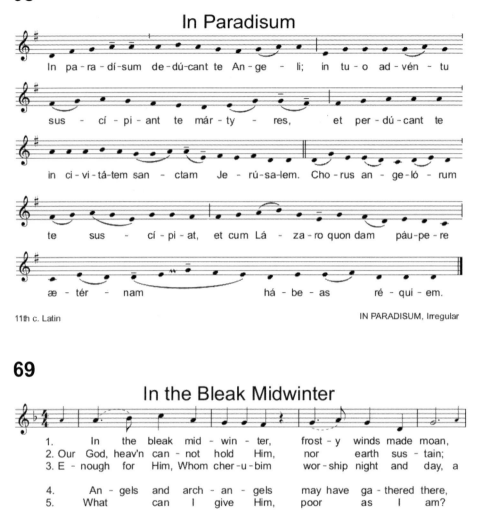

Christina Georgina Rossetti — CRANHAM, Irregular

70. In the Shadow of Your Wings

Psalm 17
Adapt. Michael O'Connor, O.P.

U Ciebie Boże, Jacek Gałuszka

Copyright © 2020 the Dominican Liturgical Center: www.dlc.foundation

71
Infant Holy, Infant Lowly

1. Infant holy, infant lowly, for His bed a cattle stall; Oxen lowing, little knowing Christ the Babe is Lord of all. Swiftly winging, angels singing, Noels ringing, tidings bringing: Christ the babe is Lord of all! Christ the babe is Lord of all!
2. Flocks were sleeping, shepherds keeping Vigil till the morning new. Saw the glory, heard the story, Tidings of a Gospel true. Thus rejoicing, free from sorrow, Praises voicing greet the morrow: Christ the babe was born for you! Christ the babe was born for you!

W Żłobie leży, Trad Polish
Tr. Edith M. Read

W ZLOBIE LEZY, 8.7.8.7.8.8.7.7.

72
Jesu, Joy of Our Desiring

1. Jesu, joy of man's desiring, Holy wisdom, love most bright; Drawn by Thee, our souls aspiring Soar to uncreated light. Word of God, our flesh that fashioned, With the fire of life impassioned Striving still to truth unknown, Soaring, dying round Thy throne.
2. Through the way where hope is guiding, Hark, what peaceful music rings; Where the flock, in Thee confiding, Drink of joy from deathless springs. Theirs is beauty's fairest pleasure; Theirs is wisdom's holiest treasure. Thou dost ever lead Thine own In the love of joys unknown.

Martin Janus;
Tr. Robert Seymour Bridges

WERDE MUNTER, 8.7.8.7.7.6.8.6.

73

Jesu Duclis Memoria

1. Je-su, dul-cus me-mó-ri-a, Dans ve-ra cor-dis gáu-di-a:
2. Nil cá-ni-tur su-á-vi-us, Nil áu-di-tur ju-cún-di-us,
3. Je-su, spes pæ-ni-tén-ti-bus, Quam pi-us es pe-tén-ti-bus!
4. Nec lin-gua va-let dí-ce-re, Nec lít-te-ra ex-prí-me-re:
5. Sis, Je-su, nos-trum gáu-di-um, Qui es fu-tú-rus præ-mi-um:

1. Sed su-per mel et óm-ni-a E-jus dul-cis præ-sén-ti-a
2. Nil co-gi-tá-tur dúl-ci-us, Quam Je-sus De-i Fí-li-us.
3. Quam bo-nus te quæ-rén-ti-bus! Sed quid in-ve-ni-én-ti-bus?
4. Ex-pér-tus po-test cré-de-re, Quid sit Je-sum di-lí-ge-re.
5. Sit nos-tra in te gló-ri-a, Per cun-cta sem-per sæ-cu-la. A-men.

Bernard of Clairvaux JESU DULCIS MEMORIA, 8.8.8.8. (L.M.)

74

Jesus, I Trust in You

Je - sys, I trust in You. You

St. Faustina Paweł Bębenek
Adapt. Christopher Mueller

Copyright © 2020 the Dominican Liturgical Center: www.dlc.foundation

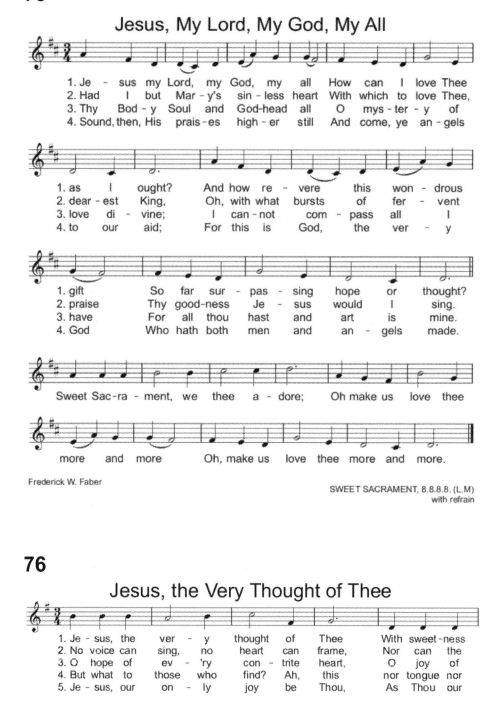

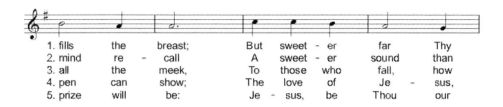

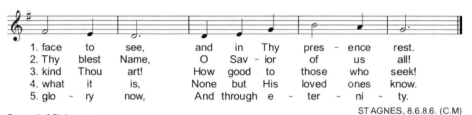

Bernard of Clairvaux;
Tr. Edward Caswall

ST AGNES, 8.6.8.6. (C.M)

77

Jesus Christ is Risen Today

Surrexit Christus hodie, 14th c. Latin;
Tr. Vs. 1-3 John Walsh, alt. Arnold;
Vs. 4 Charles Wesley

EASTER HYMN, 7.7.7.7.
with alleluias

78

Joy to the World

1. Joy to the world! the Lord is come; Let earth receive her
2. Joy to the world! the Savior reigns; Let men their songs em-
3. He rules the world with truth and grace, and makes the nations

1. King; Let ev-'ry heart pre-pare Him room and
2. ploy; While fields and floods, rocks, hills, and plains re-
3. prove the glo-ries of His righ-teous-ness and

1. heav'n and na-ture sing, and heav'n and na-ture sing, and
2. peat the sound-ing joy, Re-peat the sound-ing joy, Re-
3. won-ders of His love, and won-ders of His love, and

1. heav'n and heav'n and na-ture sing.
2. peat re-peat the sound-ing joy.
3. won-ders, won-ders of his love.

Psalm 98, Isaac Watts   ANTIOCH, 8.6.8.6. (C.M.)
                                                                 with repeat

79

Joyful, Joyful, We Adore Thee

1. Joy-ful, joy-ful, we a-dore Thee, God of glo-ry,
2. All Thy works with joy sur-round Thee, Earth and heav'n re-
3. Thou art giv-ing and for-giv-ing, Ev-er-bless-ing,
4. Mor-tals join the might-y cho-rus, Which the morn-ing

1. Lord of love; Hearts un-fold like flow'rs be-fore Thee,
2. flect Thy rays, Stars and an-gels sing a-round Thee,
3. ev-er-blest, Well-spring of the joy of liv-ing,
4. stars be-gan; Fa-ther-love is reign-ing o'er us,

1. Prais-ing Thee, their Sun a-bove. Melt the clouds of
2. Cen-ter of un-bro-ken praise. Field and for-est,
3. O-cean depth of hap-py rest! Thou our Fa-ther,
4. Broth-er-love binds man to man. Ev-er sing-ing,

1. sin and sad-ness; Drive the dark of doubt a-way;
2. vale and moun-tain, Flow'r-ing mead-ow, flash-ing sea,
3. Christ our Broth-er, All who live in love are Thine;
4. march we on-ward, Vic-tors in the midst of strife;

1. Giv-er of im-mor-tal glad-ness, Fill us with the light of day.
2. Chant-ing bird and flow-ing foun-tain Call us to re-joice in Thee.
3. Teach us how to love each oth-er, Lift us to the joy di-vine.
4. Joy-ful mu-sic lifts us sun-ward, In the tri-umph song of life.

Henry van Dyke   HYMN TO JOY, 8.7.8.7. D.

80
Lead, Kindly Light

1. Lead, kind-ly Light, a-mid the'en-cir-cling gloom, Lead Thou me on! The night is dark, and I am far from home, Lead Thou me on! Keep thou my feet! I do not ask to see The dis-tant scene; one step e-nough for me.
2. I was not ev-er thus, nor prayed that Thou Shouldst lead me on; I loved to choose and see my path; but now Lead Thou me on! I loved the gar-ish day; and, spite of fears, Pride ruled my will: re-mem-ber not past years.
3. So long Thy pow'r has blest me, sure it still Will lead me on O'er moor and fen, o'er crag and tor-rent, till The night is gone; And with the morn those an-gel fac-es smile, Which I have loved long since, and lost a-while.

Bl. John H. Newman

SANDON, 10.4.4.10.4.10.10.

81
Let All Mortal Flesh Keep Silence

1. Let all mor-tal flesh keep si-lence, And with fear and trem-bling stand; Pon-der noth-ing earth-ly mind-ed,
2. King of kings, yet born of Mar-y, As of old on earth He stood, Lord of lords, in hu-man ves-ture,
3. Rank on rank the host of heav-en Spreads its van-guard on the way, As the Light of light de-scend-eth
4. At His feet the six-winged ser-aph, Cher-u-bim with sleep-less eye, Veil their fac-es to the Pres-ence,

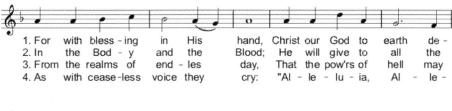
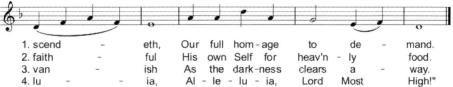

Cherubic Hymn, Liturgy of St. James, 4th c. Greek;
Tr. Gerard Moultrie

PICARDY, 8.7.8.7.8.7.

82 Lift Me Up, O Jesus

Łukasz Miśko, O.P.

Jacek Sykulski

Copyright © 2020 the Dominican Liturgical Center: www.dlc.foundation

84

Lord, Who At Thy First Eucharist

1. Lord, who at Thy first Eu-cha-rist didst pray That
2. For all Thy Church, O Lord, we in-ter-cede; Make
3. We pray Thee too for wand'r-ers from Thy fold; O
4. So, Lord, at length when sac-ra-ments shall cease, May

1. all Thy Church might be for ev-er one, Grant
2. Thou our sad di-vi-sions soon to cease; Draw
3. bring them back, good Shep-herd of the sheep, Back
4. we be one with all Thy Church a-bove, One

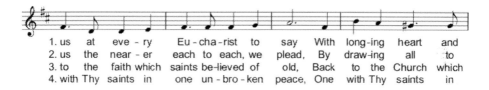

1. us at eve-ry Eu-cha-rist to say With long-ing heart and
2. us the near-er each to each, we plead, By draw-ing all to
3. to the faith which saints be-lieved of old, Back to the Church which
4. with Thy saints in one un-bro-ken peace, One with Thy saints in

1. soul, "Thy will be done." O may we all one bread, one bod-y
2. Thee, O Prince of Peace; Thus may we all one bread, one bod-y
3. still that faith does keep; Soon may we all one bread, one bod-y
4. one un-bound-ed love; More bless-ed still, in peace and love to

1.-3. be, Through this blest Sac-ra-ment of u-ni-ty.
4. be One with the Trin-i-ty in U-ni-ty.

W.H. Turton

UNDE ET MEMORES, 10.10.10.10.
with refrain

85
Lord, Who Throughout These Forty Days

1. Lord, Who throughout these forty days For us did fast and pray, Teach us with You to mourn our sins And close by You to stay.
2. As You with Satan did contend, And did the vict'ry win, O give us strength in You to fight, In You to conquer sin.
3. As You did hunger bear, and thirst, So teach us, gracious Lord, To die to self, and chiefly live By Your most holy Word.
4. And through these days of penitence, And through Your Passiontide, Forevermore, in life and death, Jesus with us abide.
5. Abide with us, that so, this life Of suff'ring o'er past, An Easter of unending joy We may attain at last.

Claudia F. Hernaman   ST. FLAVIAN, 8.6.8.6. (C.M)

86
Lord Jesus, Think on Me

1. Lord Jesus, think on me and purge away my sin; From earth-born passions set me free And make me pure within.
2. Lord Jesus, think on me, With many a care oppressed; Let me Thy loving servant be And taste Thy promised rest.
3. Lord Jesus, think on me, Amid the battle's strife; In all my pain and misery Be Thou my Health and Life.
4. Lord Jesus, think on me, Nor let me go astray; Through darkness and perplexity Point Thou the heav'nly way.
5. Lord Jesus, think on me, When floods the tempest high; When on doth rush the enemy, O Savior, be Thou nigh!
6. Lord Jesus, think on me, That, when the flood is past, I may the eternal brightness see And share Thy joy at last.
7. Lord Jesus, think on me, That I may sing above To Father, Spirit, and to Thee The strains of praise and love.

Synesius of Cyrene;
Tr. Allen W. Chatfield   SOUTHWELL, 6.6.8.6.

Love Divine, All Loves Excelling

87

1. Love divine, all loves excelling, Joy of heav'n to earth come down, Fix in us Thy humble dwelling; All Thy faithful mercies crown. Jesus, Thou art all compassion, Pure unbounded love Thou art; Visit us with Thy salvation; Enter every trembling heart.

2. Come, Almighty, to deliver, Let us all Thy life receive; Suddenly return, and never, Nevermore Thy temples leave. Thee we would be always blessing, Serve Thee as Thy hosts above, Pray and praise Thee without ceasing, Glory in Thy perfect love.

3. Finish, then, Thy new creation; Pure and spotless let us be: Let us see Thy great salvation Perfectly restored in Thee; Changed from glory into glory, Till in heav'n we take our place, Till we cast our crowns before Thee, Lost in wonder, love, and praise.

Charles Wesley

HYFRYDOL, 8.7.8.7. D.

88. My God, My God

Psalm 22
Jacek Sykulski

89. My Shepherd Will Supply My Need

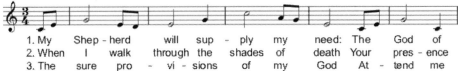

Psalm 23, Isaac Watts RESIGNATION, 8.6.8.6. (C.M.) D.

90
My Song is Love Unknown

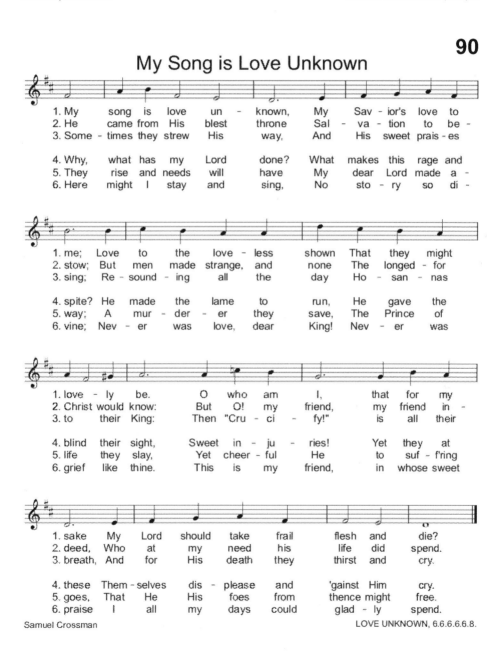

Samuel Crossman LOVE UNKNOWN, 6.6.6.6.6.8.

91
Nearer, My God, to Thee

1. Near-er my God, to Thee, Near-er to Thee. E'en though it
2. Though, like the wan-der-er, The sun gone down, Dark-ness be
3. There let the way a-ppear, Steps un-to heav'n; All that Thou
4. Then with my wak-ing thoughts, Bright with Thy praise, Out of my
5. Or if on joy-ful wing, Cleav-ing the sky, Sun, moon, and

1. be a cross That rais-eth me; Still all my song shall be,
2. o-ver me, My rest a stone; Yet in my dreams I'd be
3. send-est me, In mer-cy giv'n; An-gels to beck-on me
4. ston-y griefs, Beth-el I'll raise; So by my woes to be
5. stars for-got, Up-ward I fly; Still all my song shall be,

Near-er, my God, to Thee, Near-er my God, to Thee, Near-er to Thee.

Sarah Flower Adams

BETHANY, 6.4.6.4.6.6.6.4.

92
Now Thank We All Our God

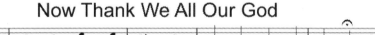

1. Now thank we all our God With heart and hands and voic-es, Who
2. O may this bount-eous God Through all our life be near us, With
3. All praise and thanks to God The Fa-ther now be giv-en, The

1. won-drous things has done, In whom His world re-joic-es; Who
2. ev-er joy-ful hearts and bless-ed peace to cheer us, To
3. Son, and Him who reigns With them in high-est heav-en, E-

1. from our moth-ers' arms Has blessed us on our way With
2. keep us in His grace, and guide us when per-plexed, And
3. ter-nal, Tri-une God, Whom earth and heav'n a-dore; For

1. count-less	gifts	of	love,	And	still	is ours	to -	day.
2. free	us	from	all	ills	In	this world	and the	next.
3. thus	it	was,	is	now,	And	shall be	ev - er -	more.

Nun danket alle Gott, Martin Rinckart
Tr. Catherine Winkworth

NUN DANKET, 6.7.6.7.6.6.6.6.

93

O Bless the Lord, My Soul

1. O	bless	the Lord, my	soul,	His	grace to	Thee pro -	claim.	And
2. O	bless	the Lord, my	soul,	His	mer - cies	bear in	mind;	For -
3. He	will	not al - ways	chide;	He	will with	pa - tience	wait;	His
4. He	par - dons all	thy	sins;	Pro - longs	thy fee - ble	breath;	He
5. He	clothes thee with His	love;	Up - holds	thee with His	truth;	And
6. Then	bless His ho - ly	Name, Whose	grace hath	made thee	whole, Whose

1. all	that	is	with -	in	me join To	bless His	ho - ly name.
2. get	not	all	His	ben - e - fits: The	Lord to	thee is kind.
3. wrath	is	ev - er	slow	to	rise, And	read - y	to a - bate.
4. heal -eth thine in -	fir - mi - ties, And	ran-soms	thee from death.
5. like	the ea - gle	he	re - news The	vi - gor	of thy youth.
6. lov - ing kind-ness	crowns thy	days; O	bless the	Lord my soul!

Psalm 103, James Montgomery

ST THOMAS (WILLIAMS), 6.6.8.6. (S.M)

94
O Breathe on Me, O Breath of God

1. O breathe on me, O Breath of God, Fill me with life a-new, That I may love what You would love, And do what You would do.
2. O breathe on me, O Breath of God, Un-til my heart is pure, Un-til with You I will one will: To do and to en-dure.
3. O breathe on me, O Breath of God, Fill me with good de-sire, 'Till all this earth-ly part of me Glows with Your ho-ly fire.
4. O breathe on me, O Breath of God, So shall I nev-er die, But live with You the per-fect life Of Your e-ter-ni-ty.

Edwin Hatch

ST. COLUMBA, 8.6.8.6. (C.M)

95
O Come, O Come, Emmanuel

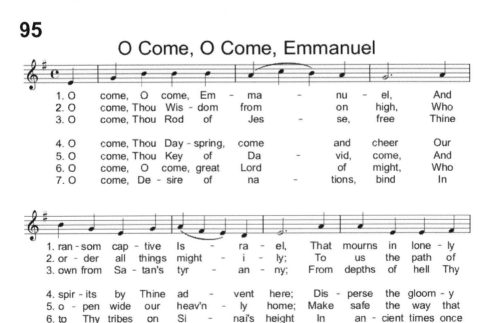

1. O come, O come, Em-ma-nu-el, And ran-som cap-tive Is-ra-el, That mourns in lone-ly
2. O come, Thou Wis-dom from on high, Who or-der all things might-i-ly; To us the path of
3. O come, Thou Rod of Jes-se, free Thine own from Sa-tan's tyr-an-ny; From depths of hell Thy
4. O come, Thou Day-spring, come and cheer Our spir-its by Thine ad-vent here; Dis-perse the gloom-y
5. O come, Thou Key of Da-vid, come, And o-pen wide our heav'n-ly home; Make safe the way that
6. O come, O come, great Lord of might, Who to Thy tribes on Si-nai's height In an-cient times once
7. O come, De-sire of na-tions, bind In one the hearts of all man-kind; Bid Thou our sad di-

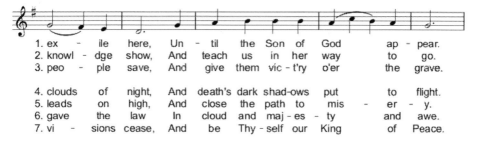

1. ex - ile here, Un - til the Son of God ap - pear.
2. knowl - dge show, And teach us in her way to go.
3. peo - ple save, And give them vic - t'ry o'er the grave.
4. clouds of night, And death's dark shad-ows put to flight.
5. leads on high, And close the path to mis - er - y.
6. gave the law In cloud and maj - es - ty and awe.
7. vi - sions cease, And be Thy - self our King of Peace.

Re - joice! Re - joice! Em - man - u - el Shall come to thee O Is - ra - el.

Veni, Veni Emmanuel, 9th c.;
Tr. John M. Neale and Henry S. Coffin

VENI EMMANUEL, 8.8.8.8. (L.M)
with refrain

96 O Come All Ye Faithful

1. O come, all ye faith-ful, joy-ful and tri-um-phant; O come ye, O come ye to Beth - le - hem.
2. God of God Light from Light, Lo! he ab - hors not the Vir - gin's womb:
3. Sing, choirs of an - gels, sing in ex-ul - ta - tion; Sing, all ye cit - i - zens of heav'n a - bove!
4. Yea, Lord, we greet Thee, Born this hap-py morn - ing; Je - sus to Thee be all glo - ry giv'n;

Ad - és - te, fi - dé - les, Læ - ti tri - um - phán - tes, Ve - ní - te, ve - ní - te in Bé - th - le - hem.

1. Come and be - hold him, born the King of an - gels;
2. Ve - ry God, be - got - ten not cre - a - ted;
3. Glo - ry to God, glo - ry in the high - est
4. Word of the Fa - ther, Now in flesh ap - pear - ing;

Na - tum vi - dé - te Re - gem an - ge - ló - rum.

O come, let us a - dore him, O come let us a - dore him, O come, let us a - dore him Christ, the Lord.

ní - te a - do - ré - mus Dó - mi - num.

Adeste Fidelis, Attr. John F. Wade
Tr. Frederick Oakeley
ADESTE FIDELES,
Irregular with refrain

97 O Come and Mourn with Me a While

1. O come and mourn with me a while; See
2. Have we no tears to shed for Him, While
3. Seven times He spoke seven words of love, And

4. O break O break hard heart of mine; Thy
5. O Love of God: O sin of man: In

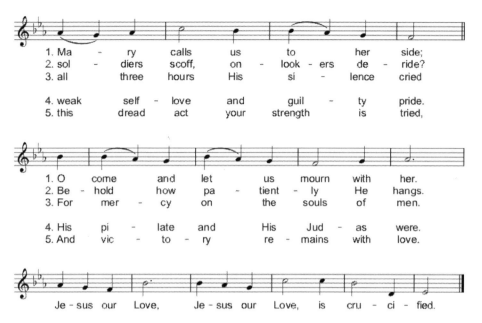

1. Mary calls us to her side;
2. soldiers scoff, on lookers deride?
3. all three hours His silence cried
4. weak self-love and guilty pride.
5. this dread act your strength is tried,

1. O come and let us mourn with her.
2. Behold how patiently He hangs.
3. For mercy on the souls of men.
4. His Pilate and His Judas were.
5. And victory remains with love.

Jesus our Love, Jesus our Love, is crucified.

William Faber   Nicola A. Montani

98

O Gates

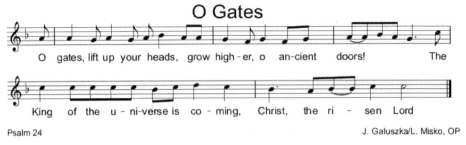

O gates, lift up your heads, grow high-er, o an-cient doors! The King of the u-ni-verse is co-ming, Christ, the ri-sen Lord

Psalm 24   J. Galuszka/L. Misko, OP

Copyright © 2020 the Dominican Liturgical Center: www.dlc.foundation

99

O Gladsome Light

1. O glad-some Light, O grace of God the Fa-ther's face,
2. Now, ere day fad-eth quite, we see the eve-ning light,
3. To Thee of right be-longs all praise of ho-ly songs,

The e-ter-nal splen-dor wear-ing; ce-les-tial, ho-ly blest,
Our wont-ed hymn out-pour-ing; Fa-ther of might un-known
O Son of God, life-giv-er; Thee, there-fore O Most High,

1. Our sav-ior Je-sus Christ, joy-ful in Thine ap-pear-ing.
2. Thee, His in-car-nate Son, and Ho-ly Ghost a-dor-ing.
3. The world doth glo-ri-fy, and shall ex-alt for-ev-er.

Phos Hilaron, 4th c. Greek;   NUNC DIMITTIS, 6.6.7.6.6.7.
Tr. Robert Bridges

100

O God, Be Gracious

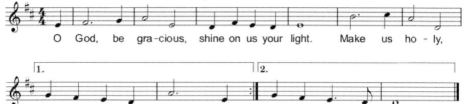

O God, be gra-cious, shine on us your light. Make us ho-ly, blame-less in your sight. O blame-less in your sight.

Ps 67
Adapted by Michael O'Connor, O.P.

Piotr Pałka

Copyright © 2020 the Dominican Liturgical Center: www.dlc.foundation

101

O God Our Help in Ages Past

Psalm 90, Isaac Watts

ST. ANNE, 8.6.8.6. (C.M)

102 O Kind Creator, Bow Thine Ear

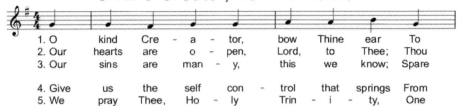
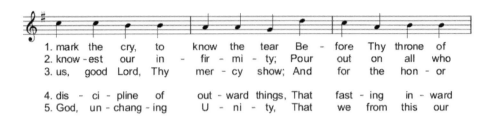
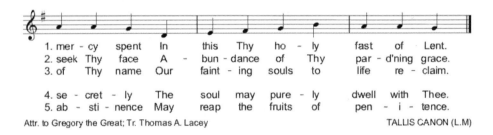

1. O kind Creator, bow Thine ear To mark the cry, to know the tear Be-fore Thy throne of mer-cy spent In this Thy ho-ly fast of Lent.
2. Our hearts are o-pen, Lord, to Thee; Thou know-est our in-fir-mi-ty; Pour out on all who seek Thy face A-bun-dance of Thy par-d'ning grace.
3. Our sins are man-y, this we know; Spare us, good Lord, Thy mer-cy show; And for the hon-or of Thy name Our faint-ing souls to life re-claim.
4. Give us the self con-trol that springs From dis-ci-pline of out-ward things, That fast-ing in-ward se-cret-ly The soul may pure-ly dwell with Thee.
5. We pray Thee, Ho-ly Trin-i-ty, One God, un-chang-ing U-ni-ty, That we from this our ab-sti-nence May reap the fruits of pen-i-tence.

Attr. to Gregory the Great; Tr. Thomas A. Lacey
TALLIS CANON (L.M)

103 O Lord, I Am Not Worthy

1. O Lord, I am not wor-thy That Thou should'st come to me, But speak the words of com-fort, My spir-it healed shall be.
2. And hum-bly I'll re-ceive Thee, The Bride-groom of my soul, No more by sin to grieve Thee, Or fly Thy sweet con-trol.
3. E-ter-nal Ho-ly Spir-it, Un-wor-thy though I be, Pre-pare me to re-ceive Him, And trust the Word to me.
4. In-crease my faith, dear Je-sus, In Thy real Pres-ence here, And make me feel most deep-ly, That Thou to me art near.

O Herr ich bin nicht würdig, 18th c. German
Tr. Anonymous
NON DIGNUS, 7.6.7.6.

105
O Sacrament Most Holy

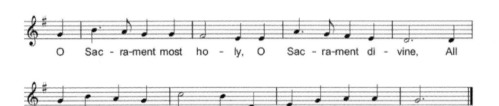

John Rodgers

FULDA MELODY, 7.6.7.6.
with refrain

106
O Sacred Head, Surrounded

1. pal - lid hue comes o'er You, The glow of life de - cays, Yet
2. ag - o - ny and dy - ing! O love to sin - ners free! Je -
3. neath Your cross a - bid - ing For - ev - er would I rest, In

1. an - gel hosts a - dore You And trem - ble as they gaze.
2. sus, all grace sup - ply - ing, O turn Your Face on me.
3. Your dear love con - fid - ing, And with Your Pres - ence blest.

Salve caput cruentatum, Attr: Bernard of Clairvaux
Tr. Henry W. Baker

PASSION CHORALE, 7.6.7.6. D

107

O Salutaris Hostia
O Saving Victim

1. O sa - lu - tá - ris Hós - ti - a, Quae
2. U - ni tri - nó - que Dó - mi - no Sit

1. O sav - ing Vic - tim o - pen wide The
2. All praise and thanks to Thee as - cend For -

1. cae - li pan - dis ós - ti - um: Bel - la pre - munt hos -
2. sem - pi - tér - na gló - ri - a, Qui vi - tam si - ne

1. gate of heav'n to man be - low; Our foes press on from
2. ev - er - more, blest One in Three; O grant us life that

1. tí - li - a, Da ro - bur, fer au - xí - li - um.
2. tér - mi - no No - bis do - net in pá - tri - a.

1. ev - 'ry side; Thine aid sup - ply; Thy strength be - stow.
2. shall not end In our true na - tive land with Thee.

St. Thomas Aquinas;
Tr. Edward Caswall

DUGUET, 8.8.8.8. (L.M)

108 O Sanctissima

1. O sanctíssima, O piíssima, Dulcis virgo María Mater amáta, intemeráta, Ora, ora pro nobis.
2. Tota pulchra es, O María et Mácula non est in te Mater amáta, intemeráta, Ora, ora pro nobis.
3. In miséria, in angústia Ora, virgo, pro nobis. Pro nobis ora in mortis hora, Ora, ora pro nobis.
4. Tu solátium et refúgium Virgo mater María: Quidquid optámus per te sperámus, Ora, ora pro nobis.

18th c. Latin — SICILIAN MARINERS, 5.5.7.5.5.7.

109 O Taste and See

O taste and see how good, how sweet is the Lord, O taste and see how good and how sweet is the Lord.

Psalm 34
Adapt. Łukasz Miśko, O.P.
Paweł Bębenek

Copyright © 2020 the Dominican Liturgical Center: www.dlc.foundation

110

Of the Father's Love Begotten

1. Of the Father's love begotten, Ere the worlds began to be,
2. At His Word the worlds were framed; He commanded; it was done:
3. He is found in human fashion, Death and sorrow here to know,
4. O that birth forever blessed When the Virgin, full of grace,
5. O ye heights of heav'n, adore Him; Angel hosts, His praises sing;
6. Christ, to Thee, with God the Father, And, O Holy Ghost, to Thee

1. He is Alpha and Omega, He the source, the ending He,
2. Heav'n and earth and depths of ocean In their three-fold order one;
3. That the race of Adam's children Doomed by law to endless woe,
4. By the Holy Ghost conceiving Bore the Savior of our race,
5. Pow'rs, dominions, bow before Him, And extol our God and King;
6. Hymn and chant and high thanksgiving And unwearied praises be:

1. Of the things that are, that have been, And that future years shall see,
2. All that grows beneath the shining Of the moon and burning sun,
3. May not henceforth die and perish In the dreadful gulf below,

4. And the Babe, the world's Redeemer, First revealed His Sacred Face,
5. Let no tongue on earth be silent, Ev'ry voice in concert ring,
6. Honor, glory, and dominion, And eternal victory,

Evermore and evermore. Amen.

Corde natus ex parentis, Prudentius;
Tr. John M. Neale and Henry W. Baker

DIVINUM MYSTERIUM, 8.7.8.7.8.7.7.

111

Of the Lord's Mercy

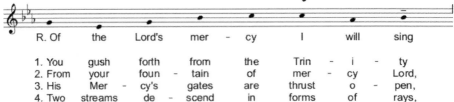

R. Of the Lord's mer - cy I will sing

1. You gush forth from the Trin - i - ty
2. From your foun - tain of mer - cy Lord,
3. His Mer - cy's gates are thrust o - pen,
4. Two streams de - scend in forms of rays,

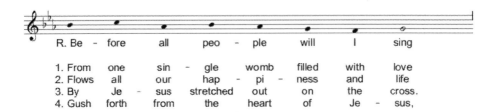

R. Be - fore all peo - ple will I sing

1. From one sin - gle womb filled with love
2. Flows all our hap - pi - ness and life
3. By Je - sus stretched out on the cross.
4. Gush forth from the heart of Je - sus,

R. It is God's great - est at - tri - bute For us un - end - ing mir - a - cle.

1. The Lord's mer - cy shown to the soul in all fullness when the veil falls.
2. Thus all crea - tures and cre - a - tion, sing out in ec - sta - cy this song.
3. Sin - ner do not doubt or de-spair, Trust mer-cy and be - come ho - ly!
4. Not for heav'n - ly host of an-gels, but for sin - ful man's sal - va - tion.

St. Faustina
Stanley

CONDITOR ALME SIDERUM, 8.8.8.8. (L.M)

Used with permission of the Marian Fathers of the Immaculate Conception of the B.V.M.

112

On Jordan's Bank

1. On Jor - dan's bank the Bap - tist's cry An -
2. Then cleansed be ev - 'ry soul from sin; Make
3. For Thou art our sal - va - tion, Lord, Our
4. To heal the sick stretch out Thy hand, And
5. All praise, e - ter - nal Son, to Thee, Whose

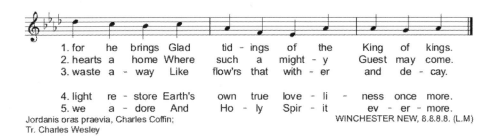

Jordanis oras praevia, Charles Coffin;
Tr. Charles Wesley

WINCHESTER NEW, 8.8.8.8. (L.M)

On This Day, O Beautiful Mother

On this day, O beau-ti-ful Mo-ther, On this day we give thee our love.

Near thee, Ma-don-na, fond-ly we hov-er, Trust-ing thy gen-tle care to prove.

1. On this day we ask to share, Dear-est Mo-ther, thy sweet care;
2. Queen of an-gels, deign to hear Lisp-ing chil-dren's hum-ble prayer;
3. Rose fo Sha-ron, love-ly flow'r Beau-teous bud of E-den's bow'r

1. Aid us ere our feet a-stray Wan-der from thy guid-ing way.
2. Young hearts gain, O Vir-gin pure, Sweet-ly to thy-self al-lure
3. Cher-ished li-ly of the vale, Vir-gin Mo-ther, Queen we hail.

Favorite Catholic Melodies, 1854

BEAUTIFUL MOTHER, 7.7.7.7.
with refrain

114

115

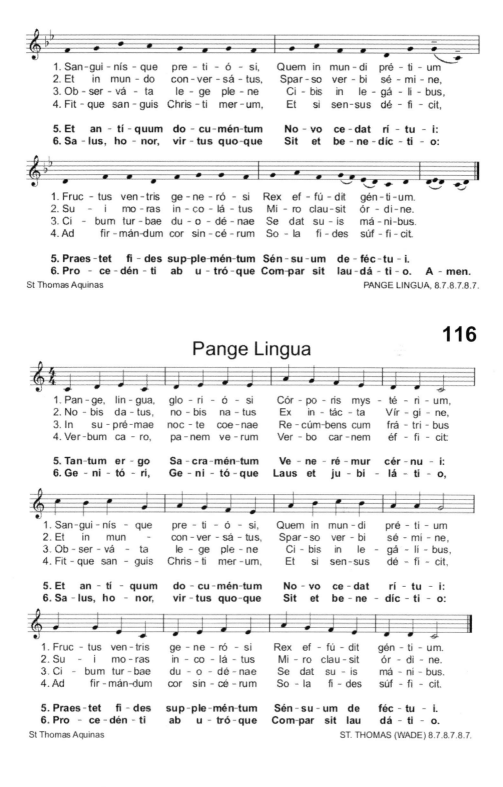

117
Panis Angelicus

1. Pa-nis an - gé - li-cus   fit   pa-nis hó - mi-num;   Dat pa-nis cæ - li-cus
2. Te tri-na Dé - i-tas   u - ná-que pós-ci-mus: Sic nos tu ví - si-ta,

1. fí - gu - ris   tér - mi - num: O   res mi - rá - bi - lis!
2. si - cut te   có - li - mus;   Per   tu - as   sé - mi-tas

1. man-dú-cat   Dó - mi-num   Pau - per,   ser - vus et   hú - mi - lis.
2. duc nos quo tén - di-mus   Ad   lu - cem quam in - há - bi - tas.

St Thomas Aquinas   SACRIS SOLEMNIIS, 12.12.12.8.

118
Parce, Domine

Par-ce, Dó-mi-ne,   par-ce pó-pu-lo   tu - o: ne in æ-tér-num i-ras-cá - ris no - bis.

1. Flec - tá - mus i - ram vín - di - cem,   Plo - ré - mus an - te   Jú - di - cem;
2. Nos - tris ma - lis of - fén - di - mus   Tu - am De - us   cle - mén - ti - am
3. Dans tem-pus ac - cep - tá - bi - le,   Da la - cri - má - rum rí - vu - lis

4. Au - di, be - ní - gne Cón - di - tor,   Nos-tras pre-ces cum flé - ti - bus
5. Scru - tá - tor al - me cór - di - um, In - fír - ma tu scus ví - ri - um;

Cla - mé - mus   o - re   súp - pli - ci,   Di - cá - mus om - nes céqr - nu - i:
Ef - fún - de no - bis dé - su - per   Re - mís - sor in - dul - gén - ti - am
La - vá - re cor - dis víc - ti - mam, Quam læ - ta'ad - ú - rat cá - ri - tas.

In hoc sa - cro je - jú - ni - o   Fu - sas qua - dra - ge - ná - ri - o.
Ad te re - vér - sis éx - hi - be   Re - mis - si - ó - nis grá - ti - am.

PARCE DOMINE, Irregular

Portal of the World's Salvation

1. Portal of the world's salvation, Lo, a virgin pure and mild, Humble-hearted, high in station, Form of beauty undefiled, Crown of earth's anticipation, Comes the Mother-maid with child.

2. Here, the serpent's pow'r subduing, See the Bush unburned by fire, Gideon's Fleece of heav'n's imbuing, Aaron's Rod of bright attire, Fair, and pure, and peace-ensuing, Spouse of Solomon's desire.

3. Jesse's Branch received its Flow'r, Mother of Emmanuel, Portal sealed and mystic Bow'r, Promised by Ezekiel, Rock of Daniel's dream, whose pow'r Smote, and lo, the image fell!

4. See in flesh so great a wonder By the pow'r of God ordained, Him, whose feet all worlds lay under, In a Virgin's womb contained; So on earth, her bonds to sunder, Righteousness from heav'n hath rained.

5. Virgin sweet, with love o'erflowing, To the hills in haste she fares; On a kindred heart bestowing Blessing from the joy she bears; Waiting while with mystic showing Time the sacred birth prepares.

6. What fair joy o'er-shone that dwelling, Called so great a guest to greet! What her joy whose love compelling Found a rest for Mary's feet, When, the bliss of time foretelling, Lo, the Voice and word did meet!

7. God most high, the heav'n's Foundation, Ruler of eternity; Jesu, Who for man's salvation Came in flesh to make us free; Ev-ermore be praise to Thee!

Mundi salus affutura, 15th c.
Tr. Laurence Housman

ST THOMAS (WADE), 8.7.8.7.8.7.

119

120

Praise, My Soul, the King of Heaven

1. Praise, my soul, the King of heaven; To His feet your tribute bring. Ransomed, healed, restored, forgiven, Evermore His praises sing. Alleluia, alleluia, Praise the everlasting King.
2. Praise Him for His grace and favor To our fathers in distress; Praise Him, still the same as ever, Slow to chide, and swift to bless. Alleluia, alleluia: Glorious in His faithfulness.
3. Father-like He tends and spares us; Well our feeble frame He knows. In His hand He gently bears us, Rescues us from all our foes. Alleluia, alleluia, Widely yet His mercy flows.
4. Frail as summer's flow'r we flourish, Blows the wind and it is gone; But while mortals rise and perish, Our God lives unchanging on, Alleluia, alleluia, Praise the high eternal One.
5. Angels, help us to adore Him, You behold Him face to face; Sun and moon, bow down before Him, Dwellers all in time and space. Alleluia, alleluia, Praise with us the God of grace.

Henry F. Lyte   LAUDA ANIMA, 8.7.8.7.8.7.

121

Praise God, From Whom All Blessings Flow

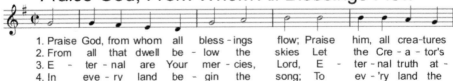

1. Praise God, from whom all blessings flow; Praise him, all creatures
2. From all that dwell below the skies Let the Creator's
3. Eternal are Your mercies, Lord, Eternal truth at-
4. In every land begin the song; To ev'ry land the

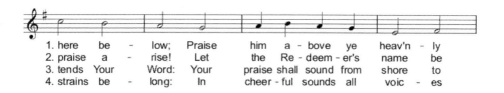

1. here be - low; Praise him a - bove ye heav'n - ly
2. praise a - rise! Let the Re - deem - er's name be
3. tends Your Word: Your praise shall sound from shore to
4. strains be - long: In cheer - ful sounds all voic - es

1. host; Praise Fa - ther, Son and Ho - ly Ghost.
2. sung Through ev - 'ry land by ev - 'ry one.
3. shore Till suns shall rise and set no more.
4. raise, And fill the world with loud - est praise.

Thomas Ken, Isaac Watts　　　　　　　　　　　　　　OLD HUNDRETH, 8.8.8.8. (L.M)

122

Praise the Lord, You Heavens, Adore Him

1. Praise the Lord, ye heav'ns, adore Him; Praise Him, angels in the height. Sun and moon, rejoice before Him; Praise Him, all ye stars of light. Praise the Lord, for He has spoken; Worlds His mighty voice obeyed. Laws which never shall be broken For their guidance He has made.

2. Praise the Lord, for He is glorious; Never shall His promise fail. God has made His saints victorious; Sin and death shall not prevail. Praise the God of our salvation; Hosts on high, His pow'r proclaim. Heav'n and earth and all creation, Laud and magnify His name.

3. Worship, honor, glory, blessing, Lord, we offer unto Thee. Young and old, Thy praise expressing, In glad homage bend the knee. All the saints in heav'n adore Thee; We would bow before Thy throne. As Thine angels serve before Thee, So on earth Thy will be done.

Psalm 148,
Vs 1-2 Anon;
Vs 3 Edward Osler

AUSTRIA, 8.7.8.7. D.

123 Praise to the Lord

1. Praise to the Lord, the Almighty the King of creation! O my soul, praise Him, for He is your health and salvation! All you who hear, now to His altar draw near; Praise Him in glad adoration.
2. Praise to the Lord, above all things so gloriously reigning; Shel-t'ring you under His wings, and so gently sustaining! Have you not seen all that is needful has been Sent by His gracious ordaining?
3. Praise to the Lord, who does prosper your work and defend you. SUrely His goodness and mercy here daily attend you. Ponder anew what the Almighty can do, If with His love He befriend you.
4. Praise to the Lord, O let all that is in me adore Him! All that has life and breath, come now with praises before Him. Let the "Amen" sound from His people again, Now as we worship before Him.

Lobe den Herren, den mächtigen König der Ehren, Joachim Neander;
Tr. Catherine Winkworth

LOBE DEN HERREN, 14.14.4.7.8.

124 Regina Caeli

Regina caeli laetare, alleluia:
Quia quem meruisti portare, alleluia:
Resurrexit, sicut dixit, alleluia:
Ora pro nobis Deum, alleluia.

12th c. Latin

REGINA CAELI (CHANT) Irregular

125

Rejoice, the Lord is King

1. Rejoice, the Lord is King! Your Lord and King adore; Rejoice, give thanks and sing, and triumph evermore;
2. Our Lord, the Savior, reigns, The God of truth and love; When He had purged our stains He took His seat above.
3. His kingdom cannot fail, He rules o'er earth and heav'n, The keys of death and hell Are to our Jesus giv'n;
4. Rejoice in glorious hope! Our Lord the Judge shall come, And take His servants up To their eternal home.

Lift up your heart, lift up your voice; Rejoice, again I say, rejoice!

Charles Wesley   DARWALLS 148, 6.6.6.6.8.8.

126

Rich in Mercy

Rich in mercy, full of compassion, patient, and unchanging is His love from age to age.

Psalm 103 Adapt. Michael O'Connor, O.P.   Jacek Sykulski

Copyright © 2020 the Dominican Liturgical Center: www.dlc.foundation

127

Salve Regina

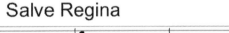

Salve, Regína, Mater misericórdiæ, vita, dulcédo, et spes nostra, salve.

Ad te clamámus éxsules fílii Hevæ, Ad te suspirámus, geméntes et flentes

in hac lacrimárum valle. Eia, ergo, advocáta nostra,

illos tuos misericórdes óculos ad nos convérte;

Et Iesum, benedíctum fructum ventris tui, nobis post hoc exsílium osténde.

O clemens, O pia, O dulcis Virgo María.

Hermann of Reichenau SALVE REGINA, Irregular, Mode 5

128
See Amid the Winter Snow

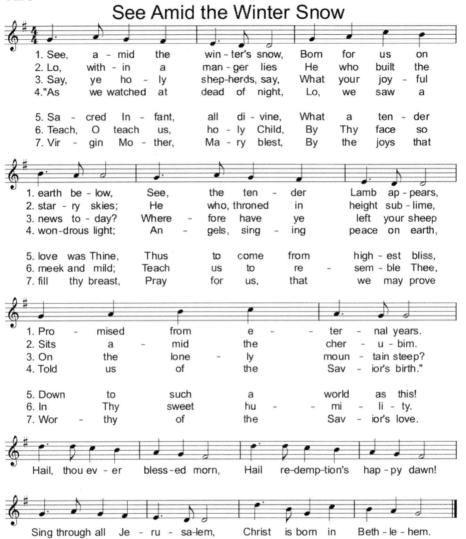

1. See, a-mid the win-ter's snow, Born for us on earth be-low, See, the ten-der Lamb ap-pears, Pro-mised from e-ter-nal years.
2. Lo, with-in a man-ger lies He who built the star-ry skies; He who, throned in height sub-lime, Sits a-mid the cher-u-bim.
3. Say, ye ho-ly shep-herds, say, What your joy-ful news to-day? Where-fore have ye left your sheep On the lone-ly moun-tain steep?
4. "As we watched at dead of night, Lo, we saw a won-drous light; An-gels, sing-ing peace on earth, Told us of the Sav-ior's birth."
5. Sa-cred In-fant, all di-vine, What a ten-der love was Thine, Thus to come from high-est bliss, Down to such a world as this!
6. Teach, O teach us, ho-ly Child, By Thy face so meek and mild; Teach us to re-sem-ble Thee, In Thy sweet hu-mi-li-ty.
7. Vir-gin Mo-ther, Ma-ry blest, By the joys that fill thy breast, Pray for us, that we may prove Wor-thy of the Sav-ior's love.

Hail, thou ev-er bless-ed morn, Hail re-demp-tion's hap-py dawn! Sing through all Je-ru-sa-lem, Christ is born in Beth-le-hem.

Edward Caswall

HUMILITY 7.7.7.7.
with refrain

129
Shepherd of Souls

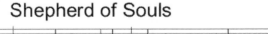

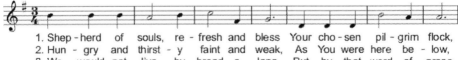

1. Shep-herd of souls, re-fresh and bless Your cho-sen pil-grim flock,
2. Hun-gry and thirst-y faint and weak, As You were here be-low,
3. We would not live by bread a-lone, But by that word of grace,
4. Be known to us in break-ing bread, But do not then de-part;
5. Lord, share with us Your love di-vine; Your bod-y and Your blood,

1. With man-na in the wil-der-ness, With wa-ter from the rock.
2. Our souls the joys ce-les-tial seek Which from Your sor-rows flow.
3. In strength of which we trav-el on To our a-bid-ing place.
4. Sav-ior a-bide with us, and spread Your ta-ble in our heart.
5. That liv-ing bread, that heav'n-ly wine, Be our im-mor-tal food.

Vs 1-3 Anon
Vs 4-5 James Montgomery

ST. AGNES, 8.6.8.6. (C.M)

130

Silent Night

1. Si - lent night! Ho - ly night! All is calm, all is bright
2. Si - lent night! Ho - ly night! Shep-herds quake at the sight;
3. Si - lent night! Ho - ly night! Son of God, love's pure light

1. Round yon Vir - gin Moth - er and child! Ho - ly In - fant so
2. Glo - ries stream from heav - en a - far; Heav'n - ly hosts sing
3. Ra - diant beams from Thy ho-ly face, With the dawn of re -

1. ten - der and mild, Sleep in heav-en-ly pea-ce, Sleep in heav-en-ly peace.
2. "Al - le - lu - ia! Christ the Sav-ior is bo-rn, Christ the Sav-ior is born."
3. deem - ing gace, Je - sus, Lord, at thy bi-rth Je-sus, Lord, at Thy birth.

Stille Nacht, heilige Nacht, Joseph Mohr
Tr. John F. Young

STILLE NACHT, 6.6.8.9.6.6.

131
Sing My Tongue the Savior's Glory

1. Sing, my tongue, the Savior's glory, Of His flesh the mystry sing; Of the Blood, all price exceeding, Shed by our immortal King, Destined for the world's redemption, From a noble womb to spring.
2. Of a pure and spotless Virgin Born for us on earth below, He as Man, with man conversing, Stayed, the seeds of truth to sow; Then He closed in solemn order Wondrously His life of woe.
3. On the night of taht Last Supper, Seated with His chosen band, He the Pascal victim eating, First fulfills the Law's command; Then as food to His Apostles Gives Himself with His own hand.
4. Word-made-Flesh, the bread of nature By His word to Flesh He turns; Wine in to His Blood He changes; What though sense no change discerns? Only be the heart in earnest, Faith her lesson quickly learns.
5. Down in adoration falling, Lo! the sacred Host we hail; Lo! o'er ancient forms departing, Newer rites of grace prevail; Faith for all defects supplying, Where the feeble senses fail.
6. To the everlasting Father, And the Son who reigns on high, With the Holy Ghost proceeding Forth from each eternally, Be salvation, honor, blessing, Might and endless majesty.

Pange, lingua, gloriosi, St Thomas Aquinas
Tr. Edward Caswall

ST. THOMAS (WADE) 8.7.8.7.8.7.

132
Sing of Mary, Pure and Lowly

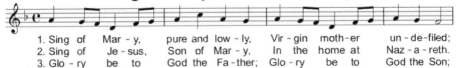

1. Sing of Mary, pure and lowly, Virgin mother undefiled;
2. Sing of Jesus, Son of Mary, In the home at Nazareth.
3. Glory be to God the Father; Glory be to God the Son;

1. Sing of God's own Son most ho-ly, Who be-came her lit-tle Child.
2. Toil and la-bor can-not wea-ry Love en-dur-ing un-to death.
3. Glo-ry be to God the Spir-it; Glo-ry to the Three in One.

1. Fair-est Child of fair-est Moth-er, God the Lord who came to earth,
2. Con-stant was the love He gave her, Though He went forth from her side,
3. From the heart of bless-ed Mar-y, From all saints the song as-cends,

1. Word made flesh, our ver-y Broth-er, Takes our na-ture by His birth.
2. Forth to preach, and heal, and suf-fer, Till on Cal-va-ry He died.
3. And the Church the strain re-ech-oes Un-to earth's re-mot-est ends.

Roland F. Palmer   PLEADING SAVIOR, 8.7.8.7 D.

133

Sing We Now of Christmas

1. O sing we now of Christ-mas, No-el sing we hear!
2. The an-gels called to shep-herds, Leave your flocks at rest;
3. In Beth-le-hem they found Him; Jo-seph and Ma-ry mild,
4. Then from the east-ern coun-try Come the kings a-far,
5. And gold and myrrh they took there, Gifts of great-est price;

1. Hear our grate-ful prais-es, To the Babe so dear.
2. Jour-ney forth to Beth-le-hem, Find the Lamb-kin blest.
3. Seat-ed by the man-ger, Watch-ing the ho-ly Child.
4. Bear-ing gifts to Beth-le-hem, Guid-ed by a star.
5. Frank-in-cense to greet the Child of par-a-dise.

Sing we No-el, the King is born, No-el! Sing we now of Christ-mas, Sing we now No-el!

Trad. French Carol   NOEL NOUVELET, 11.10.11.10.

134
Soul of Christ

Soul of Christ, sanc-ti-fy me. Blood of Christ, in-e-bri-ate me.
Bo-dy of Christ, save me

Wa-ter from the side of Christ, wash me. Pas-sion of Christ, streng-then me.

be a-part from You. From the e-vil one, de-fend me.
I my hour of death call me. And

bid that I may come close to You, And with all Your saints and an-gels

I may priase You For all e-ter-ni-ty, A - men!

14th c. Latin
Tr. Christopher Mueller

Stefan Stuligrosz
arr. Cezary Paciorek

Copyright © 2020 the Dominican Liturgical Center: www.dlc.foundation

135
Soul of My Savior

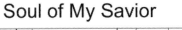

1. Soul of my Sav - ior sanc - ti - fy my breast,
2. Strength and pro - tec - tion may Thy pas - sion be,
3. Guard and de - fend me from the foe ma - lign,

1. Bod - y of Christ, be Thou my sav - ing guest,
2. O bless - ed Je - sus, hear and an - swer me;
3. In death's dread mo - ments make me on - ly Thine;

1. Blood of my Sav - ior, bathe me in Thy tide,
2. Deep in Thy wounds, Lord, hide and shel - ter me,
3. Call me and bid me come to Thee on high

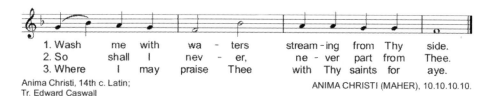

1. Wash me with wa - ters stream-ing from Thy side.
2. So shall I nev - er, ne - ver part from Thee.
3. Where I may praise Thee with Thy saints for aye.

Anima Christi, 14th c. Latin;
Tr. Edward Caswall

ANIMA CHRISTI (MAHER), 10.10.10.10.

136

Spirit Seeking Light and Beauty

1. Spir - it seek - ing light and beau - ty, Heart that long - est for Thy
2. Taste and see Him, feel and hear Him, Hope and grasp His un-seen

1. rest, Soul that ask - eth un - der - stand - ing, On - ly thus can ye be
2. hand; Tho' the dark - ness seem to hide Him, Faith and love can un - der -

1. blest. Thro' the vast-ness of cre - a - tion, Tho' your rest - less thought may
2. stand. God Who lov - est all Thy crea-tures All our hearts are known to

1. roam, God is all that you can long for, God is all His crea-tures' home.
2. Thee; Lead us thro' the land of shad-ows To Thy blest E - ter - ni - ty.

Janet Stuart

Unknown

137 Take My Life, and Let it Be

1. Take my life and let it be Con-se-crat-ed, Lord, to Thee; Take my hands and let them move At the im-pulse of Thy love, At the im-pulse of Thy love.
2. Take my feet and let them be Swift and beau-ti-ful for Thee; Take my voice and let me sing Al-ways, on-ly, for my King, Al-ways, on-ly, for my King.
3. Take my sil-ver and my gold, Not a mite would I with-hold; Take my mo-ments and my days Let them flow in cease-less praise, Let them flow in cease-less praise.
4. Take my will and make it Thine, It shall be no long-er mine; Take my heart, it is Thine own, It shall be Thy roy-al throne, It shall be Thy roy-al throne.

Frances Ridley Havergal   7.7.7.7.7.7.

138 Take Up Your Cross

1. "Take up your cross," the Sav-ior said, "If you would My dis-ci-ple be; Take up your cross with will-ing heart, And hum-bly fol-low af-ter Me."
2. Take up your cross, let not its weight Fill your weak spir-it with a-larm; His strength shall bear your spir-it up, And brace your heart and nerve your arm.
3. Take up your cross, heed not the shame, Nor let your fool-ish pride re-bel; Your Lord for you en-dured the cross, To save your soul from death and hell.

Charles W. Everest, alt   ERHALT UNS HERR, 8.8.8.8. (L.M)

139

The Advent of Our King

1. The ad-vent of our King Our prayers must now em-ploy And we must hymns of wel-come sing In strains of ho-ly joy.
2. The ev-er-last-ing Son In-car-nate deigns to be; Him-self a ser-vant's form puts on To set His ser-vants free.
3. Daugh-ter of Zi-on, rise To meet thy low-ly King, Nor let thy faith-less heart de-spise The peace He comes to bring.

Instantis adventum Dei, Charles Coffin;
Tr. John Chandler

ST THOMAS (WILLIAMS), 6.6.8.6. (S.M.)

140

The Angel Gabriel

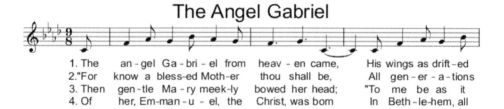

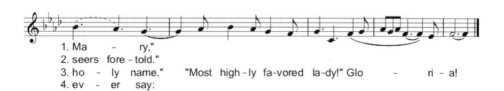

1. The an-gel Ga-bri-el from heav-en came, His wings as drift-ed snow, his eyes as flame "All hail," said he, "thou low-ly maid-en Ma - ry,"
2. "For know a bless-ed Moth-er thou shall be, All gen-er-a-tions laud and hon-or thee, Thy Son shall be Em-man-u-el, by seers fore-told."
3. Then gen-tle Ma-ry meek-ly bowed her head; "To me be as it pleas-es God!" she said. "My soul shall laud and mag-ni-fy His ho-ly name." "Most high-ly fa-vored la-dy!" Glo - ri - a!
4. Of her, Em-man-u-el, the Christ, was born In Beth-le-hem, all on a Christ-mas morn; And Chris-tian folk through-out the world will ev - er say:

Birjina gaztetto bat zegoen,
trad. Basque

GABRIEL'S MESSAGE, 10.10.12.10.

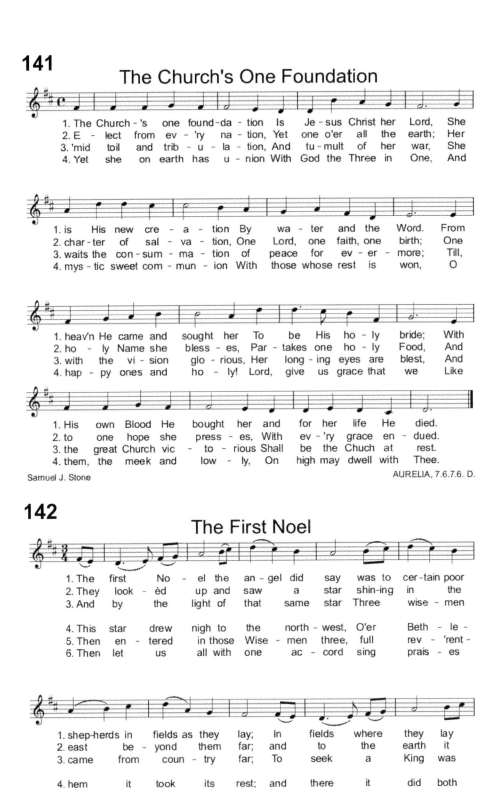

18th c. English   THE FIRST NOWELL, Irregular

143
The King of Love My Shepherd Is

Psalm 23, Henry W. Baker   ST. COLUMBA, 8.7.8.7.

144 The King Shall Come When Morning Dawns

1. The King shall come when morning dawns, And light triumphant breaks; When beauty gilds the eastern hills, And life to joy awakes.
2. Not as of old a little child To bear, and fight, and die, But crowned with glory like the sun That lights the morning sky.
3. The King shall come when morning dawns, And earth's dark night is past; O haste the rising of that morn: That day shall ever last.
4. And let the endless bliss begin, By weary saints foretold, When right shall triumph over wrong, And truth shall be extolled.
5. The King shall come when morning dawns, And light and beauty brings: Hail, Christ the Lord! Your people pray, Come quickly, King of kings.

Anon. Greek; Tr. John Brownlie MORNING SONG, 8.6.8.6. (C.M)

145 The Royal Banners

1. The royal banners forward go, The
2. There while He hung, His sacred side, By
3. Fulfilled is now what David told, In
4. O tree of glory, tree most fair, Or -
5. Upon its arms, like balance true, He
6. To you, eternal Three in One, Let

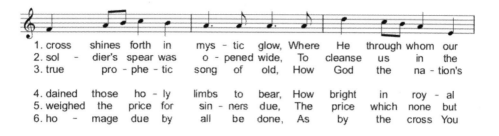

1. cross shines forth in mys - tic glow, Where He through whom our
2. sol - dier's spear was o - pened wide, To cleanse us in the
3. true pro - phe - tic song of old, How God the na - tion's
4. dained those ho - ly limbs to bear, How bright in roy - al
5. weighed the price for sin - ners due, The price which none but
6. ho - mage due by all be done, As by the cross You

1. flesh was made, In that same flesh our ran - som paid.
2. pre - cious flood Of wa - ter min - gled with His blood.
3. king should be; For God is reign - ing from the tree.
4. robe it stood, The pur - ple of a Sa - vior's blood!
5. He could pay, And spoiled the spoi - ler of his prey.
6. did re - store, So rule and guide us e - ver - more.

Vexilla Regis, Venantius Fortunatus, 6th ct.
Tr. John M. Neale

Paweł Bębenek

Copyright © 2020 the Dominican Liturgical Center: www.dlc.foundation

146
The Snow Lay on the Ground

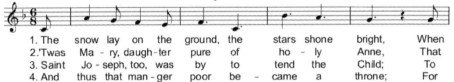

1. The snow lay on the ground, the stars shone bright, When
2. 'Twas Ma-ry, daugh-ter pure of ho-ly Anne, That
3. Saint Jo-seph, too, was by to tend the Child; To
4. And thus that man-ger poor be-came a throne; For

1. Christ our Lord was born on Christ-mas night. Ve - ni - te ad - o -
2. brought in - to this world the God made man. She laid Him in a
3. guard Him, and pro - tect His mo - ther mild; The an - gels hov-ered
4. He whom Ma - ry bore was God the Son. O come, then, let us

1. re - mus Do - mi - num. Ve - ni - te ad - o - re - mus Do - mi - num. Ve-
2. stall at Beth - le - hem; The ass and ox - en shared the roof with them.
3. round, and sang this song, Ve - ni - te ad - o - re - mus Do - mi - num.
4. join the heav'n-ly host; To praise the Fa-ther Son and Ho - ly Ghost.

ni - te ad - o - re - mus Do - mi - num. Ve - ni - te ad - o - re - mus Do - mi - num.

Anon.

VENITE ADOREMUS, 10.10.10.10.
with refrain

147
The Strife is O'er

Al - le - lu - ia! Al - le - lu - ia! Al - le - lu - ia!

1. The strife is o'er, the bat - tle done;
2. The pow'rs of death have done their worst;
3. The three sad days are quick - ly sped;
4. He closed the yawn - ing gates of hell;
5. Lord, by the stripes which wound - ed Thee,

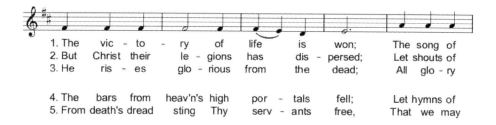

1. The vic-to-ry of life is won; The song of tri-umph has be-gun:
2. But Christ their le-gions has dis-persed; Let shouts of ho-ly joy out-burst:
3. He ris-es glo-rious from the dead; All glo-ry to our ris-en Head! Al-le-lu-ia!

4. The bars from heav'n's high por-tals fell; Let hymns of praise His tri-umphs tell!
5. From death's dread sting Thy serv-ants free, That we may live, and sing to Thee:

Finita iam sunt proelia, 12th c. Latin
Tr. Francis Pott

VICTORY, 8.8.8.
with alleluias

148 There's a Wideness in God's Mercy

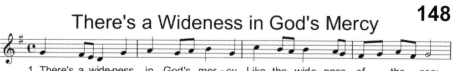

1. There's a wide-ness in God's mer-cy Like the wide-ness of the sea;
2. For the love of God is broad-er Than the meas-ure of our mind;
3. Souls of men, why will you scat-ter Like a crowd of fright-ened sheep?

1. There's a kind-ness in His jus-tice, Which is more than lib-er-ty.
2. And the heart of the E-ter-nal Is most won-der-ful-ly kind.
3. Fool-ish hearts, why will you wan-der From a love so true and deep?

1. There is plen-ti-ful re-demp-tion In the blood that has been shed;
2. If our love were but more sim-ple, We should take Him at His word;
3. There is wel-come for the sin-ner, And more grac-es for the good;

1. There is joy for all the mem-bers In the sor-rows of the Head.
2. And our lives would be all sun-shine In the sweet-ness of our Lord.
3. There is mer-cy with the Sav-ior; There is heal-ing in His Blood.

Frederick W. Faber

IN BABILONE, 8.7.8.7. D.

149
Ubi Caritas

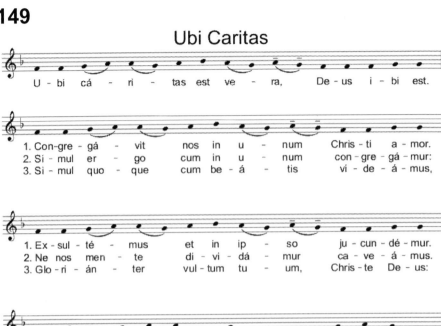

U - bi cá - ri - tas est ve - ra, De - us i - bi est.

1. Con-gre - gá - vit nos in u - num Chris - ti a - mor.
2. Si - mul er - go cum in u - num con - gre - gá - mur:
3. Si - mul quo - que cum be - á - tis vi - de - á - mus,

1. Ex - sul - té - mus et in ip - so ju - cun - dé - mur.
2. Ne nos men - te di - vi - dá - mur ca - ve - á - mus.
3. Glo - ri - án - ter vul - tum tu - um, Chris - te De - us:

1. Ti - me - a - mus et a - mé - mus De - um vi - vum.
2. Ces-sent iúr - gi - a ma - líg - na ces - sent li - tes.
3. Gáu - di - um quod est im - mén - sum at - que pro - bum,

1. Et ex cor-de di - li - gá - mus nos sin - cé - ro.
2. Et in mé - di - o nos-tri sit Chris-tus De - us.
3. Sæ-cu - la per in-fin-ní - ta sæ - cu - ló - rum. A - men.

Trad. Latin UBI CARITAS, Irregular

150
Veni Creator

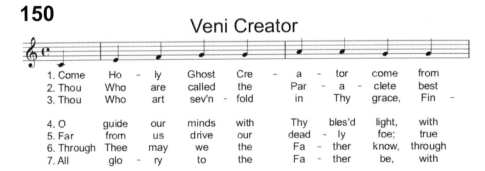

1. Come Ho - ly Ghost Cre - a - tor come from
2. Thou Who are called the Par - a - clete best
3. Thou Who art sev'n - fold in Thy grace, Fin -

4. O guide our minds with Thy bles'd light, with
5. Far from us drive our dead - ly foe; true
6. Through Thee may we the Fa - ther know, through
7. All glo - ry to the Fa - ther be, with

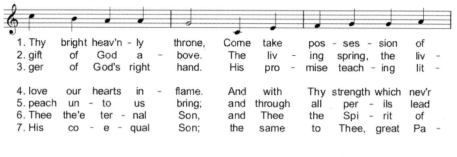

1. Thy bright heav'n-ly throne, Come take pos-ses-sion of
2. gift of God a-bove. The liv-ing spring, the liv-
3. ger of God's right hand. His pro-mise teach-ing lit-
4. love our hearts in-flame. And with Thy strength which nev'r
5. peach un-to us bring; and through all per-ils lead
6. Thee the'e-ter-nal Son, and Thee the Spi-rit of
7. His co-e-qual Son; the same to Thee, great Pa-

1. our souls, and make them all Thy own.
2. ing fire, Sweet unc-tion and true love.
3. tle ones to speak and un-der-stand.
4. de-cays con-firm our mor-tal frame.
5. us safe be-neath Thy sa-cred wing.
6. Them both, Thrice-bless-ed Three in One.
7. ra-clete, while end-less ag-es run.

Tallis   Tallis

Veni Creator Spiritus

151

1. Ve-ni Cre-á-tor Spí-ri-tus, Men-tes tu-ó-rum ví-si-ta:
2. Qui dí-ce-ris Pa-rá-cli-tus, Do-num De-i al-tís-si-mi,
3. Tu sep-ti-fór-mis mú-ne-re, Dex-træ De-i tu dí-gi-tus,
4. Ac-cén-de lu-men sén-si-bus, In-fún-de a-mó-rem cór-di-bus,
5. Hos-tem re-pél-las lón-gi-us, Pa-cém-que do-nes pró-ti-nus:
6. Per te sci-á-mus da Pa-trem, Nos-cá-mus at-que Fí-li-um
7. De-o Pa-tri sit gló-ri-a, Et Fí-li-o, qui a mór-tu-is

1. Im-ple su-pér-na grá-ti-a Quæ tu cre-ás-ti péc-to-ra
2. Fons vi-vus, ig-nis, cá-ri-tas, Et spi-ri-tá-lis ún-cti-o.
3. Tu ri-te pro-mís-sum Pa-tris, Ser-mó-ne di-tans gút-tu-ra.
4. In-fír-ma nos-tri cór-po-ris Vir-tú-te fir-mans pér-pe-ti.
5. Duc-tó-re sic te præ-vi-o, Vi-té-mus om-ne nó-xi-um.
6. Te u-tri-ús-que Spí-ri-tum Cre-dá-mus om-ni tém-po-re.
7. Sur-ré-xit, ac Pa-rá-cli-to, In sæ-cu-ló-rum sæ-cu-la. A-men.

Rabanus Maurus   VENI CREATOR SPIRITUS, 8.8.8.8. (L.M.)

152

Wake, Awake for Night is Flying

1. Wake, a-wake, for night is fly - ing; The watch-men on the
2. Zi - on hears the watch-men sing - ing, And all her heart with
3. Now let all the heav'ns a - dore You And saints and an - gels

1. heights are cry - ing: A - wake, Je - ru - sa - lem, at last!
2. joy is spring - ing; She wakes, she ris - es from her gloom;
3. sing be - fore You, With harp and cym-bal's clear - est tone;

1. Mid-night hears the wel - come voic - es And at the thrill - ing
2. For her Lord comes down all glo - rious, The strong in grace, in
3. Of one pearl each shin - ing por - tal, Where we are with the

1. cry re - joic - es; Come forth, O vir - gins, night is past; The
2. truth vic - to - rious. Her star is ris'n, her light is come. O
3. choir im - mor - tal Of an - gels round Your daz - zling throne; No

1. Bride-groom comes, a - wake; Your lamps with glad - ness take; Al - le - lu - ia! And
2. come, O bless - ed One, God's own be - lov - ed Son: Al - le - lu - ia! We
3. eye has seen, no ear has yet at - tained to hear Joys e - ter - nal, but

1. for His mar - riage feast pre - pare For you must go and meet Him there.
2. fol - low You and en - ter through Where You have bid us sup with You.
3. we re - joice and sing to You Our hymn of joy, for ev - er new.

Wachet auf, ruft uns die Stimme, Phil;lip Nicolai
Tr. Catherine Winkworth

WACHET AUF, 8.9.8.8.9.8.6.6.4.4.4.8.

153

We Three Kings

1. We three kings of Orient are; Bearing gifts we traverse afar Field and fountain, Moor and mountain, Following yonder star.
2. Born a King on Bethlehem's plain, Gold I bring to crown him again, King forever, Ceasing never Over us all to reign.
3. Frankincense to offer have I; Incense owns a Deity nigh; Prayer and praising voices raising. Worshipping God on high.
4. Myrrh is mine; its bitter perfume Breathes a life of gathering gloom; Sorr'wing, sighing, Bleeding, dying, Sealed in the stone cold tomb.
5. Glorious now behold him arise, King and God and Sacrifice; "Alleluia, Alleluia!" Sounds through the earth and skies.

Refrain:
O star of wonder, star of night, Star with royal beauty bright; Westward leading, still proceeding, Guide us to thy perfect light.

John H. Hopkins, Jr.

KINGS OF ORIENT, 8.8.8.6.
with refrain

154

Welcome Bread of Life

1. Welcome, Bread of Life, where God, beyond all measure, Maker of the heav'ns and earth, is found: our treasure! Welcome, wondrous Drink, which to desirous minds is Fully satisfying.
2. Welcome, flowing fountain, full of heav'n's abundance, For we know that God is held within your substance; You tell all mankind of His eternal pow'r; His graces you show ever.
3. Welcome, golden manna, from the heav'ns descending; In our hearts a taste delightful and unending; Nothing in the world surpasses it in flavor, Lightness, or savor.
4. Welcome, precious fruit from Eden's perfect Garden; Those who taste the Tree of Life, when granted pardon, Yee! who eat that fruit shall fear of death no longer; God's love is stronger.
5. Welcome, happiness, when God alone my heart fills; Welcome, blest relief, to all who face this world's ills; I am seeking You with sweetest tears and sighing; For You I'm crying.

17th-cent. Polish;
Tr Łukasz Miśko, OP &
Christopher Mueller, OK (2015)

P. Bębenek

Copyright © 2020 the Dominican Liturgical Center: www.dlc.foundation

155

What Child Is This?

1. What Child is this Who, laid to rest, On Mary's lap is
2. Why lies He in such mean estate, Where ox and ass are
3. So bring Him incense, gold and myrrh, Come peasant, king to

1. sleep-ing? Whom an - gels greet with an - thems sweet, While
2. feed-ing? Good Chris - tians, fear, for sin - ners here The
3. own Him; The King of kings sal - va - tion brings, Let

1. shep-herds watch are keep-ing? This, This is Christ the King, Whom
2. si - lent Word is plead-ing. Nails, spear shall pierce Him through, The
3. lov - ing hearts en - throne Him. Raise, raise a song on high, The

1. shep-herds guard and an - gels sing; Haste, Haste, to
2. cross be borne for me, for you. Hail, Hail the
3. Vir - gin sings her lull - a - by. Joy, joy for

1. bring Him laud, The Babe, the Son of Mar - y.
2. Word made flesh, The Babe, the Son of Mar - y.
3. Christ is born, The Babe, the Son of Mar - y.

William C. Dix

GREENSLEEVES, 8.7.8.7.
with refrain

156
What Wondrous Love is This

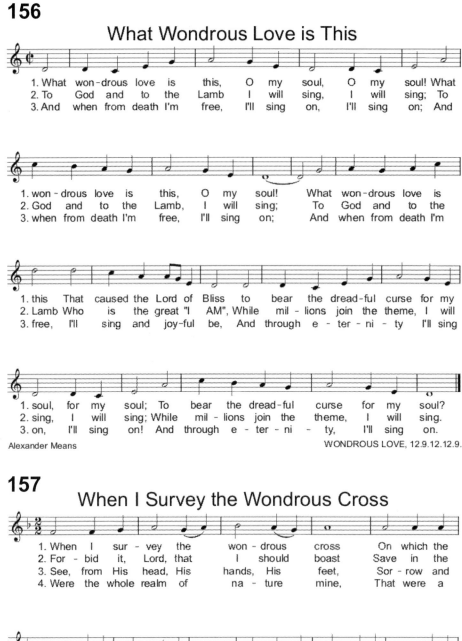

1. What wondrous love is this, O my soul, O my soul! What wondrous love is this, O my soul! What wondrous love is this That caused the Lord of Bliss to bear the dreadful curse for my soul, for my soul; To bear the dreadful curse for my soul?
2. To God and to the Lamb I will sing, I will sing; To God and to the Lamb, I will sing; To God and to the Lamb Who is the great "I AM", While millions join the theme, I will sing, I will sing; While millions join the theme, I will sing.
3. And when from death I'm free, I'll sing on, I'll sing on; And when from death I'm free, I'll sing on; And when from death I'm free, I'll sing and joyful be, And through eternity I'll sing on, I'll sing on! And through eternity I'll sing on.

Alexander Means

WONDROUS LOVE, 12.9.12.12.9.

157
When I Survey the Wondrous Cross

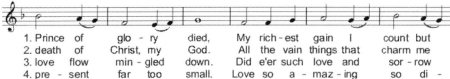

1. When I survey the wondrous cross On which the Prince of glory died, My richest gain I count but
2. Forbid it, Lord, that I should boast Save in the death of Christ, my God. All the vain things that charm me
3. See, from His head, His hands, His feet, Sorrow and love flow mingled down. Did e'er such love and sorrow
4. Were the whole realm of nature mine, That were a present far too small. Love so amazing so di-

1. loss,   And   pour con - tempt   on   all   my   pride.
2. most,   I   sac - ri - fice   them   to   His   Blood.
3. meet?   Or   thorns com - pose   so   rich   a   crown?
4. vine,   De - mands my   soul,   my   life,   my   all.

Isaac Watts HAMBURG 8.8.8.8.

158

Within Thy Sacred Heart

1. With - in Thy Sa - cred Heart, dear Lord, My anx - ious thoughts shall
2. Say on - ly Thou hast par - doned me, Say on - ly I am
3. Ah! Why is not my love for Thee Un - bound - ed past con -
4. Ah, Je - sus! if love's trust - ing prayer Seem not too bold to

1. rest. I nei - ther ask for life nor death. Thou know - est what is best.
2. Thine. In all things else dis - pose of me. Thy Ho - ly Will is mine.
3. trol? A - las! my heart o - bey - eth not The im - pulse of my soul!
4. Thee, Place Thy own heart with - in my breast; Love Thou Thy - self for me!

Irish prayer Corner

159

Ye Sons and Daughters

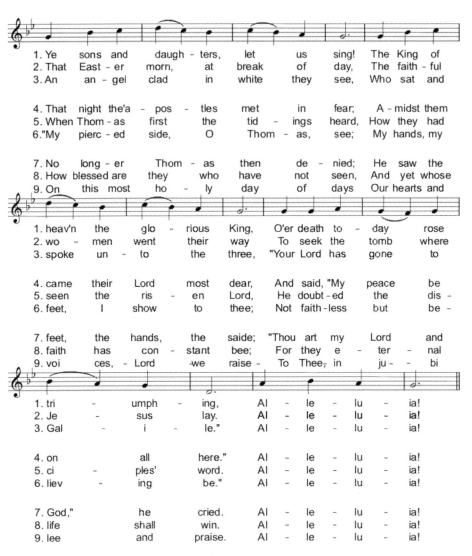

1. Ye sons and daughters, let us sing! The King of heav'n the glorious King, O'er death today rose triumphing, Alleluia!
2. That Easter morn, at break of day, The faithful women went their way To seek the tomb where Jesus lay. Alleluia!
3. An angel clad in white they see, Who sat and spoke unto the three, "Your Lord has gone to Galilee." Alleluia!
4. That night the'apostles met in fear; Amidst them came their Lord most dear, And said, "My peace be on all here." Alleluia!
5. When Thomas first the tidings heard, How they had seen the risen Lord, He doubted the disciples' word. Alleluia!
6. "My piercèd side, O Thomas, see; My hands, my feet, I show to thee; Not faithless but believing be." Alleluia!
7. No longer Thomas then denied; He saw the feet, the hands, the saide; "Thou art my Lord and God," he cried. Alleluia!
8. How blessed are they who have not seen, And yet whose faith has constant bee; For they eternal life shall win. Alleluia!
9. On this most holy day of days Our hearts and voices, Lord we raise To Thee, in jubilee and praise. Alleluia!

O filii et filiae, Attr. Tisserand; Tr. John M. Neale

O FILI ET FILIAE, 8.8.8. with alleluias

160

Ye Watchers and Ye Holy Ones

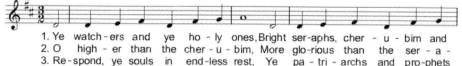

1. Ye watch-ers and ye ho-ly ones, Bright ser-aphs, cher-u-bim and
2. O high-er than the cher-u-bim, More glo-rious than the ser-a-
3. Re-spond, ye souls in end-less rest, Ye pa-tri-archs and pro-phets
4. O friends, in glad-ness let us sing, Su-per-nal an-thems ech-o-

1. thrones, Raise the glad strain, Al-le-lu ia! Cry out, do-min-ions, prince-doms,
2. phim, Lead their prais-es, Al-le-lu ia! Thou bear-er of th'e-ter-nal
3. blest, Al-le-lu-ia! Al-le-lu ia! Ye ho-ly twelve, ye mar-tyrs
4. ing, Al-le-lu-ia! Al-le-lu ia! To God the Fa-ther, God the

1. pow'rs, Vir-tues, arch-an-gels, an-gels' choirs:
2. Word, Most gra-cious, mag-ni-fy the Lord. Al-le
3. strong, All saints tri-um-phant, raise the song.
4. Son, And God the Spir-it Three in One.

lu-ia! Al-le-lu-ia! Al-le-lu-ia! Al-le-lu-ia! Al-le-lu-ia!

Athelstan Riley LASST UNS ERFREUEN, 8.8.8.8. (L.M.) with alleluias

INDEX

Mass Parts begin on Page 1

Title	Song #
Tis Good Lord to Be Here	1
A Thrilling Voice by Jordan Rings	2
Abide With Me	3
Adoro Te Devote	4
Again We Keep this Solemn Fast	5
All Creatures of Our God and King	6
All Glory Laud and Honor	7
All Hail the Power of Jesus' Name	8
All People that On Earth Do Dwell	9
All You Who Seek a Comfort Sure	10
Alleluia, Alleluia	11
Alleluia, Sing to Jesus	12
Alma Redemptoris Mater	13
Angels We Have Heard on High	14
As With Gladness Men of Old	15
At the Lamb's High Feast We Sing	16
Attende Domine	17
Ave Maria chant	18
Ave Regina Caelorum	19
Ave Verum Chant	20
Away in a Manger	21
Be Joyful Mary	22
Be Still My Soul	23
Be Thou My Vision	24
Beautiful Savior	25
Behold the Dwelling of God	26
Bring Flowers of the Rarest	27
By the Blood that Flowed From Thee	28
Christ the Lord is Risen Today	29
Christus Vincit	30
Come Down O Love Divine	31
Come Holy Ghost	32

Come My Way My Truth My Life	33
Come Thou Almighty King	34
Come Thou Long Expected Jesus	35
Comfort Comfort O My People	36
Creator of the Stars of Night	37
Crown Him with Many Crowns	38
Daily Daily Sing to Mary	39
Draw Near and Take the Body of the Lord	40
Drop, Drop Slow Tears	41
Faith of Our Fathers	42
Faithful Cross the Saints Rely On	43
Firmly I Believe and Truly	44
For All the Saints	45
For the Beauty of the Earth	46
Forty Days and Forty Nights	47
From all that Dwell Below the Skies	48
God is Love Let Heaven Adore Him	49
God Whose Almighty Word	50
Godhead Here in Hiding	51
Guide Me O Thou Great Redeemer	52
Hail, O Bright Star of Ocean	53
Hail Holy Queen Enthroned Above	54
Hail the Day that Sees Him Rise	55
Hark! A Thrilling Voice is Calling	56
Hark! the Herald Angels Sing	57
Hear Us O Mighty Lord	58
Holy, Holy, Holy	59
Holy God We Praise Thy Name	60
Holy Patron Thee Saluting	61
How Firm a Foundation	62
I Heard the Voice of Jesus Say	63
I Know that My Redeemer Lives	64
I Sing the Mighty Power of God	65
Immaculate Mary	66
Immortal Invisible God Only Wise	67
In Paradisum	68

In the Bleak Midwinter	69
In the Shadow of Your Wings	70
Infant Holy Infant Lowly	71
Jesu, Joy of Man's Desiring	72
Jesu Dulcis Memoria	73
Jesus I Trust in You	74
Jesus My Lord My God My All	75
Jesus the Very Thought of Thee	76
Jesus Christ is Risen Today	77
Joy to the World	78
Joyful Joyful We Adore Thee	79
Lead Kindly Light	80
Let all Mortal Flesh Keep Silence	81
Lift Me Up O Jesus	82
Lo How a Rose E'er Blooming	83
Lord Who at Thy First Eucharist	84
Lord Who Throughout These Forty Days	85
Lord Jesus Think on Me	86
Love Divine All Love's Excelling	87
My God, My God	88
My Shepherd Will Supply My Need	89
My Song is Love Unknown	90
Nearer My God to Thee	91
Now Thank We All Our God	92
O Bless the Lord My Soul	93
O Breathe on Me O Breath of God	94
O Come O Come Emmanuel	95
O Come All Ye Faithful	96
O Come and Mourn with Me a While	97
O Gates	98
O Gladsome Light	99
O God Be Gracious	100
O God Our Help in Ages Past	101
O Kind Creator Bow Thine Ear	102
O Lord I am not Worthy	103
O Pure Virgin	104

Title	Page
O Sacrament Most Holy	105
O Sacred Head Surrounded	106
O Salutaris Hostia	107
O Sanctissima	108
O Taste and See	109
Of the Father's Love Begotten	110
Of the Lord's Mercy	111
On Jordan's Bank	112
On This Day O Beautiful Mother	113
Once in Royal David's City	114
Pange Lingua	115
Pange Lingua Wade	116
Panis Angelicus	117
Parce Domini	118
Portal of the World's Salvation	119
Praise God From Whom All Blessings Flow	120
Praise My Soul the King of Heaven	121
Praise the Lord You Heavens Adore Him	122
Praise to the Lord	123
Regina Caeli	124
Rejoice the Lord is King	125
Rich in Mercy	126
Salve Regina	127
See Amid the Winter Snow	128
Shepherd of Souls	129
Silent Night	130
Sing My Tongue the Savior's Glory	131
Sing of Mary	132
Sing We Now of Christmas	133
Soul of Christ	134
Soul of My Savior	135
Spirit Seeking Light and Beauty	136
Take My Life and Let it Be	137
Take Up Your Cross	138
The Advent of Our King	139
The Angel Gabriel	140

The Church's One Foundation	141
The First Noel	142
The King of Love My Shepherd Is	143
The King Shall Come When Morning Dawns	144
The Royal Banners	145
The Snow Lay on the Ground	146
The Strife is O'er	147
There's a Wideness in God's Mercy	148
Ubi Caritas	149
Veni Creator	150
Veni Creator Spiritus	151
Wake, Awake for Night is Flying	152
We Three Kings	153
Welcome Bread of Life	154
What Child is This	155
What Wondrous Love	156
When I Survey the Wondrous Cross	157
Within Thy Sacred Heart	158
Ye Sons and Daughters	159
Ye Watchers and Ye Holy Ones	160

Made in the USA
Columbia, SC
25 November 2024

4137c965-dc1c-4e47-8f2a-b8fccb873331R01